2012 Wisdom of The Elohim

The Complete Virtual Serenity 12-Part Teaching Series Transcript

2012 Wisdom of The Elohim

The Complete Virtual Serenity 12-Part Teaching Series Transcript

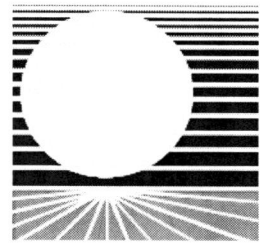

As Channeled by Rebecca Jernigan
Commentary by Marshall Masters

Your Own World Books
Silver Springs, NV USA

virtualserenity.com
yowbooks.com
kolbrin.com

Copyright

No part of this book may be reproduced or transmitted in any form or by any means, graphic, electronic, or mechanical, including photocopying, recording, taping, or by any information storage retrieval system, without the written permission of the publisher.

2012 Wisdom of The Elohim: The Complete Virtual Serenity 12-Part Teaching Series Transcript
Channeled Teachings by Rebecca Jernigan
Commentary by Marshall Masters

Your Own World Books
Virtual Serenity Teaching Series
Audio/Video Transcripts with Commentary
First Edition – January 2009

Trade Paperback
ISBN-10: 1-59772-081-X
ISBN-13: 978-1-59772-081-6

YOUR OWN WORLD BOOKS
an imprint of Your Own World, Inc.
Silver Springs, NV USA
virtualserenity.com
yowbooks.com
kolbrin.com
SAN: 256-1646

Notices
Every effort has been made to make this book as complete and as accurate as possible and no warranty or fitness is implied. All of the information provided in this book is provided on an "as is" basis. The authors and the publisher shall not be liable or responsible to any person or entity with respect to any loss or damages arising from the information contained herein.

Trademarks
All terms mentioned in this book that are known to be trademarks or service marking have been capitalized. Your Own World, Inc. cannot attest to the accuracy of this information and the use of any term in this book should not be regarded as affecting the validity of any trademark or service mark.

Table of Contents

About This 12-Part Video Teaching Series

Throughout the annals of human history there, has always been a consistent trend. The human experience of a sixth sense: our precious ability to search beyond the horizon for sustenance, shelter and safety. Given to us by the Creator for the greater good, many leave it to waste, like unharvested crops of golden wheat and grain.

A few possess the courage to harvest what they can, and this series of teachings was created especially for them. To help enable them to harvest that which they already know and can feel within the grasp of their own spiritual senses.

To you beloved seekers of light, herein is knowledge to help you to understand the purpose of your own psychic gifts. Use it for the greater good, and your sixth sense will guide you to harvests where all may share in the bounty, in a spirit of love and charity.

If you have not yet awakened your own natural gifts, the knowledge presented here will help you understand those who have. Work with them for the common good, and shower them with love and compassion. In return, you too will awaken your own gifts.

Regardless of your natural abilities, be prepared to challenge your beliefs of the world today, for the world of tomorrow shall be unimaginable. A passing world so horrifying that the gift of seeing beyond the horizon must, as it always has for the ancients, become humanity's saving grace once again.

There is much to survive for, as this dark future is only a brief, transitional phase within a further-reaching transformation of humanity. Beyond it will come a day when all shall enjoy the magnificent harvests of a new and more enlightened future.

All 12 programs in this teaching series can be freely downloaded via the Internet, in both audio and video formats.

Virtual Serenity	**URL**
◢ Web Site	virtualserenity.com
◢ Free Videocasts	video.virtualserenity.info
◢ Free MP3 Audios	audio.virtualserenity.info

Acknowledgments

First and foremost, I wish to thank The Elohim and Rebecca Jernigan, through whom they channeled their invaluable teachings.

This project represents a distillation of over a year of intensive research. It would not have been possible without the active involvement and consultations of yowusa.com co-founders Janice Manning and Jacco van der Worp, MSc. Likewise, my special thanks to fellow 2012 researcher, Echan Deravy, for his helpful insights and encouragement.

While developing this series, we also asked yowusa.com subscribers and our planetxforecast.info message board moderators to critique the teachings. As a result, their feedback helped shape the commentary in this series. We appreciate their efforts and valuable contributions.

Research efforts such this do require financial assistance. For this reason, I wish to express my deep gratitude to our many patrons and yowusa.com subscribers, for making this vital work possible.

Foreword by Marshall Masters

While many view 2012 as a looming cataclysm, I've come to see it as a looming transformational event. Yes, the path is bumpy but for humanity as a whole, the final destination is certainly worthy of our greatest hopes.

This holistic paradigm is a reflection of my own existential process of study and contemplation. One that humbled me with the realization of how very little we know. Yet, every knowledge quest begins with a first step, and mine occurred in 1999.

It was then that I began writing on Earth changes and space threats. During the subsequent decade-long prolific journey, I created and published numerous books, web sites, videos, podcasts and radio shows on 2012 and Planet X.

Each is different in style and substance; all are nonetheless based in the same science-oriented approach. However, what makes this project different from all these others is that it encapsulates my own personal holistic transformation.

Yet at the outset, my only goal was to achieve a rational understanding of what we're facing in the years ahead.

Upon reflection, I now remember these as my left-brained validation days, although there was certainly nothing pleasant about them.

They were never joyous memories, because coming to understand the hardships humanity will face in the years to come is a heavy burden. Oftentimes I've longed to be proven patently wrong so that I could abandon my work.

What happened instead was that we discovered an ever-increasing convergence of collaborating data. The data we obtained from historical accounts, prophecy and the present day scientific findings published by NASA and other traditional science sources kept snapping together like the pieces of a horrific puzzle.

Consequently, an enduring sense of duty pushed me on, and what actually enabled me to trudge forward was a simple, hopeful notion.

That being the expectation that upon reaching a particular threshold, enough data and findings would exist to satisfy my own need for certainty. From that point on, I could then coast along for a while, without having to grind through the process of authoring a peer review paper. A few articles on the Internet would suffice.

All those who contribute articles yowusa.com have gladly labored over the years to freely share research findings with others. Our mission is not to prove anything to anyone, but rather, to encourage others to seek out knowledge that resonates with them and to take action on it in a manner of their own choosing.

Unlike traditional scientists who must perpetually elbow their way to the funding trough, this has always been a personal search for the truth for me. Consequently, I've never had to worry about defending sacred cows or the possibility of losing my funding because the ego-thin sensibilities of some faceless bureaucratic power broker happen to become inexplicably offended.

This in turn has given me a free hand to pursue the truth wherever it may lead, and in late 2004, my journey finally brought that elusive validation threshold into sight. Sensing a moment of arrival, I half-expected the quintessential "ah-ha" moment. Then I could finally ease my foot off the research pedal and coast along for a while.

In retrospect, it was a naïve notion that was brusquely retired, having served its purpose. As with all of man's creations, it had its own expiration date, as coasting along was never what the universe had in mind for me. Not by a long shot.

Straight away, and right upon the heels of my "ah-ha" moment, came the most brutal question of all. "Now that you get it, Marshall, how are you going to get through it?"

In an instant, what had been yesterday's goal of validation had suddenly and unexpectedly morphed into a monstrous new topic: the survival and coming evolution of our species.

"Forget the coasting dream, laddie," I remember telling myself. It was back to work, and the obvious next question was where do I begin — once again?

When it comes to surviving 2012, the obvious starting place centers one upon the material issues of survival. Beans, rice, condensed milk, home built survival bunkers, water filters, self-protection and so forth. This is because we're quite unlike ancient indigenous peoples who know better, simply because their ancient ancestors have survived previous global cataclysms.

In today's consumer society, surviving 2012 is not about what's in our hearts for most people. Rather, it is about what is in their bunkers.

As clever as we may think we are, the brutal truth is that Western rational thinkers have no track record to speak of. In fact, when it comes to surviving a global cataclysm, all they've really got are piles of right-sounding ideas, theories and guesstimates. Furthermore, one wonders about how many of them can pass the simple math smell test. For example, comparing the number of lifeboat seats available on the Titanic against the number of souls on board

'Twas hubris that foundered the Titanic — not ice. Yet, in a mindless replay of history, our leaders are intentionally and consistently turning a deaf ear to the compassionate warnings of indigenous peoples, the very people who have a proven and successful track record of surviving global cataclysms!

This is why researching these material, shopping solutions became a dry and unsatisfying process for me. Much like eating a 500-lb. Caesar salad without the dressing, or the croûtons for that matter. Now matter how much you chomp down, there's always something missing. I call it the "K-Mart survival fallacy."

Like the enticing calls of the mythical Greek Sirens, this modern fallacy easily lures all those who want to assuage their fears for the future into a false sense of security. All they need to do is to purchase the latest, new and improved, ultra-max blue light surviving global cataclysm special. Then, they stuff it somewhere in the back of their garages, so they can go about their usual business without a care in the world.

The consumer logic is flawless. If the worst happens, they've got the solution in their garages. Just heat and serve. Conversely, if the worst fails to happen, the freshness dates on their ultra-max blue light caches will expire. Then, like insurance policies we never file claims on, they can then write off their blue light investments as legitimate peace of mind expenditures.

Mind you, this is not to diminish the need for material preparations. They are necessary, but then again, everything has its place.

The real blue light reality that we all need to come to grips with is that we're all facing the same global cataclysm — together. Not one that will last a few days or weeks, but rather, one that will most certainly plague us for years, like the mother of all cosmic train wrecks.

Ergo, no matter how many blue light specials people have cached away in their garages, there will come a point in time when the survival stores will all be gone.

So what will they do then? Lie down, and say, "Dumb luck that" and patiently wait to die from complications arising from a back-ordered attack of post-traumatic consumerism?

No doubt many will go that way, but not me, and I hope the same goes for you too! Never forget, that 2012 is about choice. Never! Never! Never forget!

Speaking for myself, I choose to get through this because I'm in it for the species. Each day that I can survive without being a burden on others shall offer me a new opportunity to make a difference. Thankfully, I know I'm not alone in this.

Quiet and withdrawn from the vulgar hubris of mockery, I've begun to see the growing signs of a veritable army of lightworkers. Committed to service to others, they're out there in greater numbers than most could possibly imagine. They walk softly and carry big hopes.

Who are they? They are the meek, and to understand what that really means, look up the etymology of the word in the dictionary. When you see how the ancients used the term, you see a world view that is entirely different from contemporary usage. It is something more.

Absent of resentment and possessing the patience of Job, the meek will endure 2012, long after the aggressive have consumed each other with their shortsighted, dog-eat-dog antics. Then, the meek will continue to quietly soldier on through thick and thin.

Their compassion and humility will draw them to a greater destiny, though getting there will be terribly difficult. Yet upon their faces will shine the dawn of a new future, and upon their backs shall rest the loving hand of the Creator.

I must be frank. As a secular researcher, my decade of intensive study into the coming global cataclysm has led me to a simple if not begrudging realization. Psalms 25:8, is not an allegory. *The Meek Shall Inherit the Earth* is a scientifically precise prediction!

However, the meek shall not be anointed, selected or righteously affiliated. Rather, they shall come from many walks of life and faiths, and each and every one will choose to walk their own path with the Creator.

These are the meek that shall inherit the Earth, and they will endure. After the blue skies and sweet waters return, they will collectively reflect upon the foibles of our many flawed belief systems and say "never again!"

Then, they will go on to build a new and better world. A compassionate and brave one that will provide the noble foundation our species needs to reach to the stars. Yet, that is tomorrow, and today is today.

My today is therefore shaped by the somewhat modest goal of pushing back against a futuristic tide of what I call "the lost tears." Seldom a day passes, when I do not touch these tears in my thoughts, and so they task me.

In the coming years, the children, the innocents, will certainly cry from fear and hunger. Yet, these unfortunate tears of suffering shall only be one facet of an inevitable reality. We must accept that and comfort them as best we can.

What I'm talking about is a different kind of kind of tears, the kind that defy simple comfort, which is why I call them the lost tears. As the emotional safe havens of the innocents begin to implode, rivulets of lost tears will trickle down through the layers grime masking their rosy, red cheeks.

This will be a time when adults who've avoided any effort to prepare themselves emotionally or spiritually for the coming tribulation will suddenly find themselves up against a bitter fate. Their casual "I'll cross the bridge when I come to it" bravado strategies will leave them and their innocents in tow stranded before a shattered bridgehead in some distant and obscure future.

Then, the worst happens for the innocents. The adults, who were once were the bedrock and beacons of their lives, become completely unhinged. Worse yet, some will lose their humanity altogether, and become predatory and vicious. When this happens, the innocents will know that they are truly alone, and their lost tears shall flow as the bitterest waters of humanity.

Assuming that all that I do, write and say prevents just one lost tear — that is good. And in that case, one can never be enough. This is what compels me to publish these wisdom teachings of The Elohim.—*Marshall Masters*

Part 1

—

Our Prophetic Dreams

Prophetic dreams are very personal things. They leave us with sticky imprints of what is to be, for there is a purpose to them. They task us explore our feelings for keys to inner wisdom. Although we collect many keys during our lives, few ever use them to unlock the doors of knowledge. This series therefore begins with the story of one man's life, which was forever changed by the turn of a key.

Series Introduction

Marshall's Motto

Destiny comes to those who listen,
and fate finds the rest.

So learn what you can learn,
do what you can do,
and never give up hope!

Marshall Masters: Each night in our dreams we see things that are soon forgotten. Sometimes we wake up in the middle of the night to write them down, so as to remember them. But then there are dreams that take us to the future and what do we see? Cataclysm and suffering on an unimaginable scale — and us and those whom we love — in the midst of it as well.

Unlike ordinary dreams, these we remember with perfect clarity, just as we remember a first kiss. A moment in time that becomes a part of the fabric of our life as each detail becomes enmeshed in our consciousness — forever.

These prophetic dreams: these horrific dreams. They awaken us in then middle of the night and we know that we can never forget them, nor can we live with the memory of them, until we know their meaning. Only then, can we protect ourselves, and those we hold dear.

You have arrived at this moment not by chance, but by cosmic design. You have questions, and perhaps the answers offered in this program will help give meaning to your prophetic dreams and visions.

With meaning comes the peace of mind you seek and need. Your journey reaches far beyond these teachings, but for now, you are here, and this is where we shall begin.

Prophetic Dreams
and Visions

Creation 4:3: "There were
some who struggled harder,
because their desires were
turned Godward, and they
were called The Children of
God."

—*The Kolbrin Bible*

Marshall Masters: Dreams and visions come through a connection to all life around us. Here in this world and elsewhere. It is not an accident that we have these dreams, for they are given to us by loving guides, who want us to prevail in the difficult times ahead. Accept these dreams as gifts of love. Use them as gifts of love. Use them to survive.

The Elohim are distant friends, but we are connected to them as we are connected to all life in the universe. In this teaching series, the Elohim share a basic level of knowledge, to help you understand the meaning of your prophetic dreams in a survival sense.

We cannot survive as one, but we can survive as many. To think as the many, we must love the many and struggle for ourselves — those whom we love and our species — as many in the one.

The guides speak for the many and your visions were given you so that you can walk the path of the teacher. To give confidence, understanding and meaning to others, so they may face their fears with bravery and compassion for others.

This is a noble undertaking and a calling to brave souls who seek the meanings of their dreams.

The personal meaning of your dreams is simple. It is to live with love and courage. This is the only meaning you need to know for yourself, but you were not given these prophetic visions and dreams for yourself. They were given to you, so that you would seek their meaning and then teach them to those who seek to leave the darkness of fear behind them.

This is the purpose of your dreams. That you believe them, their meaning and this purpose, is for you and only you, to decide.

My Own
Prophetic Dream

Silver Bough 2:12: "When the
implications of my fate
awoke knowledge in my
heart, I wept, in the spirit-lit
darkness."

—The Kolbrin Bible

Marshall Masters: To teach is to lead by example and so I must
share with you my own prophetic vision. A dream that haunted
me for months; many decades ago when I was a younger man
living in Texas. A prophetic vision so important, it was given to
me night after night in precisely the same manner. Eventually it
became a permanent remembrance so the visions would survive
intact.

In this vision I was shown a place I never knew, but sensed
that I would come to know. A place far away from me, but very
near a major city. A city I did not know, but would likewise become known to me in the fullness of time.

It was a brutal dream, filled with death and quiet misery. A
place where the suffering came to live or die, resigned to either
fate. A place where the business of hope, was no more; and just
hope itself was something beyond the next step.

My vision always began the same way, with the terrible skies of volcanic eruptions and meteor impacts. Black-streaked and sullen it cast an eerie light across a barren and lifeless landscape. It was here; thorough a narrow pass in the foothills bordering this great metropolis, the weary and forlorn came to meet their fate.

What I saw was a place of final choice, a triage center, as bureaucrats would call it. There, the suffering chose to surrender their lives peacefully or to continue the struggle for life, in what had become a barren and brutish world.

Overlooking this place of choosing, I watched as they descended through the narrow pass into a dry lake bed.. There to be sorted into areas set aside for the business of living and dying.

I knew not the name of this place, but I saw it with such detail that to this day, I still vividly remember warm gritty puffs of wind on my face and the tint of the sky that would not yield me even the slightest trace of blue.

My visions of this place persisted until I was so beset by it that I developed hemorrhoids from the stress and a hasty surgery was required. Then, the guides, who'd given me this dreadful vision night after night for months, finally gave me peace from it.

Not the peace of forgetfulness though I spent countless years trying to wipe it from my mind, but to no avail. It persisted in the distant reaches of my memory, for a purpose I neither understood nor wanted to understand.

That was until I moved to northern California from the dream place of my vision in Texas. I was drawn to this area by a material purpose without the hint that I'd actually follow a completely different destiny path. This would be revealed to me just after the dawn of the new millennium.

It was then I discovered this place of I'd first seen in Texas, and which I'd tried so often and so vigorously, to forget.

Oddly, I'd passed by this place for several years without knowing it, but that would change after I began writing my first novel, Godschild Covenant, Return of Nibiru. Through it, I would find the meaning of an irrepressible vision given to me decades ago, half a country way.

Godschild Covenant Discovery

Creation 2:23: "Where is there a wiser father than the Spirit of God, or a better mother than Earth?"

—The Kolbrin Bible

Marshall Masters: When I began writing Godschild Covenant, I struggled with the manuscript. It was as though I was an archer who could not hit anywhere near the center of the target and each chapter seemed like an arrow that missed its mark. No matter how carefully I aimed, it was as though I could not focus on the target.

It was then that synchronicity brought me a passing acquaintance. Supportive of my efforts, he read my early manuscript and quickly saw the gap in it and volunteered to help me close it.

He invited me to meet him at a spot where he liked to visit during his moments of reading and contemplation. A place known to those who live in the southern parts of the San Francisco bay area, as the Lexington reservoir in Los Gatos, California. A place I'd passed countless times during my daily commutes between the Silicon Valley of San Jose to the coastal area where I lived. This time was different, because I would follow him along a road I'd never traveled before.

He led me around the shoreline to a spot overlooking the calm waters of the Lexington reservoir, and the low mountain range that separated it from the vast metropolis just beyond. Off to my left there was the narrow pass through which I'd seen emaciated and diseased people wrapped in tattered linens, struggling on foot to this place of dying.

It was then that I stood in the very place where I'd first stood in my vision decades past in a city thousands of miles away and I was there now. Each detail of the land was exactly as before, save for the precious green and blue that now make it a place of beauty. My heart was so broken I collapsed like a rag doll and wept.

When I finally arose, I knew that I found the place of my vision as well as my purpose. After that, the words of my novel Godschild Covenant, Return of Nibiru poured out from me, like water from an eternal wellspring. It was a process of ecstasy such as only writers can know and in it, I embedded the substance of my prophetic vision. Yet, one question remained unanswered.

Decades earlier I'd seen this place as barren and dusty, devoid of the tranquil blue waters that filled this reservoir. How it could become a dry and dusty bowl? That simply escaped me. Early on in Texas where I'd first seen this place, and later in California after I actually found it, I never had the answer to the question. So, I did as I've learned to do with mysteries. Place them in a clear jar, put it on the shelf, and wait for synchronicity to provide me with a label.

That empty first went up on the shelf in January 2003, with the publication of the first edition of Godschild Covenant. Then five years later, in the summer of 2008, synchronicity delivered the label and again I was not the first to see it.

Rather, it was my dear wife Yelena. Following our usual southward journey to our home near the Monterey coast we drove past the Lexington Reservoir as always and this is when she noticed that it was being drained.

The official explanation for draining the reservoir is that to allow for engineering improvements, and that it will remain drained until 2010, assuming it can be refilled at that time.

How a prophetic vision could drive me through the years towards this place of great significance is something that can only be important to you, not to me. What is important to me is the burden of responsibility that compels me to do what I do.

If you have been given the responsibility to teach, then how and why is for you to decide. If you believe your purpose, then teach what has been shown you.

The Elohim can only offer ideas and concepts to bind your vision with passionate teachings that will help bring comfort the desperate souls of those who seek you and those like you, in the days to come. They will be in great need of teachers. Teachers of light: Teachers of love. This is the purpose of your prophetic dreams and they are your calling. Should you choose to accept them as I have accepted mine, I wish you peace and strength.

Part 2

—

We are The Elohim

We are who we are, just as you are who you are. In this realization we are all connected. This is the essential message the Elohim wish us to understand. That we are all equally connected with them as they are with humanity, through a common goal of peace and enlightenment. Their message is about loving each other as a way to survive, so that we may prosper with dignity and evolve with nobility. It is their purpose for being and their message to us through these teachings.

Speaking with The Elohim

Scrolls 16:7: "This is the
secret of life: Man lives in
God and God lives in man.
This answers all questions."

—*The Kolbrin Bible*

Marshall Masters: Hello. I'm Marshall Masters. I am the founder and publisher of the Your Own World USA website, yowusa.com web site, along with co-founders, Jacco van der Worp and Janice Manning. We've been using this site since 1999 to publish articles and interviews regarding 2012-related issues. Although our research was fruitful, science had only given us answers to physical world questions, and could not take us beyond that.

This limitation was unacceptable because our studies showed us that we're approaching an evolutionary event. Yes, terribly tragic in one sense: but magnificent in another. To better understand these dynamics, we needed to go beyond the conventional methods, into the realm subjective analysis: A field of study generally avoided by traditional scientists.

As independent researchers, we are not encumbered by economic and peer standing concerns, which leaves us completely free to go wherever the truth leads. So in 2006, we embarked upon a serious investigation of channeled messages and our first step was to develop a protocol for our subjective study to insure reliable results.

The protocol we developed for our study is based on three principles. First, no one single voice is omnipotent. Two, statistical trends are favored over specifics and three; the internal logic of each message is validated so as to minimize the effect of channel filtering by the sensitive.

We interviewed many entities of various kinds and through multiple sensitives using this protocol over an 18-month period. The statistical results were surprisingly similar to the hundreds of emails and letters we've received over the years from people reporting their own prophetic dreams and visions, such as two suns in the sky, tsunamis, earthquakes, and of course Nibiru, or what is more commonly known as Planet x.

The guides we found most helpful and consistent were The Elohim, whom we interviewed through Rebecca Jernigan, a popular syndicated radio host. Rebecca has channeled the Elohim since she was a little girl and is finely attuned to their communication methods.

Of the many excellent sensitives we used in our study, Rebecca proved to be the most accurate and consistent. It was with this in mind, that we invited The Elohim to share this teaching series through Rebecca. What you will hear in each of the teaching in this series is the voice of The Elohim, unedited and delivered as-is.

And now, I have the honor to introduce to you The Elohim, as spoken through the voice of sensitive and channeler, Rebecca Jernigan. Join us now as they introduce themselves and their purpose for these teachings.

We are The Elohim

The Elohim: Welcome. We are the Elohim, and we are here to speak to you today of who we are and our purpose in serving you. Through this media event of audio, we should explain to you that our sole purpose here is simply to share information and to be supportive of those beings on the Earth plane going through this time ahead and forward.

There is much information written about us, the Elohim, in your books, and we would say to you, the most of what is said comes from a partial knowledge of who we are. For we are multidimensional beings, as you are, and through the course of our communication with you, you too shall learn what it means to be truly multidimensional. Again, we say to you, our purpose here is to educate, to inform and to be in service.

We mentioned we are written about in many books. We are mentioned throughout history that is known and unknown. We are on hieroglyphs, within caves, within structures below ground that have yet to be discovered. We have been written about in the book that you call *The Holy Bible*. We have been written about in the discovery of the Keys of Enoch, the Dead Sea Scrolls. We have been written about in every religion, every non-religion, we have been spoken about. We would tell you that we have not always in human history of the Earth been known as the Elohim. You have heard through the course of your experience on this Earth plane the Council, the Watchers, the Founders. The list goes on. Invariably, it will be the Council of Seven, Twelve or Thirteen. Or the Watchers – again Seven, Twelve or Thirteen.

We present ourselves to an individual or a group when they are in the space of opening, of awareness, on a deeper level. We are not capable of making changes within the group or individual receiving the information, for that is being filtered. We have no reason to cause harm to a physical body, which is what would happen to a physical body, should we interject what they are seeing, what they are comprehending and what they are filtering.

There are many of you lightworkers out there, who are also in service, in service to yourselves, to humanity and to the Creator. We commend you for acknowledging; you're in service to others. We would simply ask those who know of their journey forward to take responsibility for self and for others, as you have agreed.

We have been here forever. We have *not* been incarnated; however, we *have* shared many times with beings incarnated on this planet and others. So, we are fully aware of the challenges and the joys of being in a physical place. We will keep this in context with how it relates to being incarnate on the Earth plane. We have no other agenda to be here, other than to share with you our knowledge, in hopes that you will absorb it, you will understand it and you will become that, which you are to become in the times ahead. Until we meet again.

We are Multi-dimensional Beings

Scrolls 9:6: "The clouds obscuring the lesser lights, darken the face of wisdom."

—*The Kolbrin Bible*

Marshall Masters: In this first introduction The Elohim told us that we are multidimensional beings, just like them. The only difference is that we've incarnated in physical bodies, whereas they have never done so. Given that, what is a multidimensional being? That is a fair question and so let me answer in the context of our overall study findings.

In grammar school, we're taught to see ourselves as existing in a physical, three-dimensional universe. Later in college, gifted mathematicians tell us that their complex equations are revealing a universe with more dimensions than we can count on both hands.

The question then becomes, how do we want to experience these others dimensions: Through abstract mathematical equations, or better yet, to experience them directly, through dreams and altered states of consciousness. While not all of us can do the math, we each can, and do experience these other dimensions directly.

In these other dimensions, time and motion as we known them in this reality are different and this depends on the dimension to which we travel. Shamans and spiritualists travel to these other dimensions by intent, but most of us do it unintentionally during our sleep. Consequently, what we briefly glimpse in these other dimensions often become fitful dreams that are soon forgotten.

However, when we our spirit is intentionally guided by another spirit into another dimension, we have enough time to see what we must learn, so as to can remember it accurately. The spirit entities that guide to our appointed visions and truths do so with careful love and attention. When we show our appreciation for them through love, we bring both them and ourselves closer to the creator.

In our next lesson, The Elohim will share the basic concept of awareness. The most crucial skill you can possess as it will keep you one step ahead of trouble.

Part 3

—

Survival Awareness

Why is it that so many fall: while a mysterious few escape the same fate? For some, it is chance and play. However, for others in this small minority, it is the direct consequence of their own survival senses. They see beyond the horizon and can sense where dangers lurk, as well as where sustenance and safety await. This is a powerful talent given to us by our creator. To awaken it, one need only needs to begin the simple process of awareness.

Be the Flag

Morals and Precepts 45:11-12: "A friend is one who silences your opponents when you are not there."

—*The Kolbrin Bible*

Marshall Masters: We all share a desire to be part of something greater than ourselves and often employ symbols to bind our connections to one another. The most obvious symbols we use are flags, such as the flags of our peoples, nations and all they represent. When we salute a flag, that very act of recognition connects to others who likewise value the same flag.

In this common thread of awareness, we find brotherhood and sisterhood with those who share our same values and beliefs.

Yet when we salute a flag, we actually see a symbol that is separate and apart from us. The connection we feel is elsewhere than the symbol, even though it is a repository of our connectedness: But what about the flag itself?

Infused with so many connections, what would it feel like to be connected, yet separated by distance from all those sensing a connection through you to others?

Now imagine that you are not saluting that cherished flag, but rather, that you're a thread of life within it. One that senses the environment about itself and all the emotions connected to and through you directly. With each of puff of wind, comes the added sensation of a common movement and a shared spirit within the body of the flag itself.

It is in this sense that we can be connected to our world through awareness. Not to be apart from it as we are with our symbols, but to see ourselves as being a single thread of life within it, touched by the elements of nature about us, and the feelings of all those connected to us.

Once you become aware enough to see yourself as a living thread within the flag of our world and our species, you will then have a connection to the awareness of those who have endured past global cataclysms.

They now salute us thorough their teachings and we shall return their salute, by carrying the flag of our world through the next global cataclysm. This is why this first teaching of the Elohim about awareness, is the most important of all.

Survival Awareness

The Elohim: We will begin with what we think is the first and foremost important message that we can be giving you, which is awareness. We understand that this term has been used quite frequently and quite often, much like the terms that get overused , such as metaphysical, New Age, etc. But awareness is more than just the statement of becoming aware of your surroundings. It's becoming aware of self. It's becoming aware of who you are. This is going to be very important in the days, weeks, months and years ahead, for being aware is more about vibrating with the natural energies that we are all made of – that you are all made of, which means we must take that responsibility. a key word here.

I see many of you shirking from that word, responsibility. But it does not mean that it has to have a negative connotation to it. It simply means taking the step to find out who you are. What makes you tick?

You know, we do not look at you as broken; however, we look at you as works in progress. And in the – grand scheme of things, where you are at on your line of growth, we can all become better than we are. So this is not about judgment where you're at, only taking the responsibility that there's more to do for self than what you've done up to this point.

There are many of you out there who are already along your path, and for that, we commend you; however, we would tell you it's to continue to take it a step further. Push your own envelope. Take the responsibility. Seek out others. They may be able to open doors and windows within the soul of the spirit of who you are to bring to you that awareness.

Many of you out there feel as if you have grown to a point where you are comfortable where you're at. You have the knowledge of the changes coming forward. You speak and communicate with your own guides very well. There's still more to be done. There's still more to raise your level of awareness, to let go of those things that no longer serve you in this reality.

We are being very, very adamant that this is the first step in this process, the awareness. You know, there is help out there; there is assistance out there, and I hear many of you saying, "Well, I'm fine. I have all the knowledge that I need." Well, not yet, because you haven't brought it into awareness. The awareness, awareness of how intricate we are all connected has not hit many of you yet. The awareness, the joy and bliss and happiness can be yours on a day-to-day basis, because raising the awareness also raises your vibration. When your own vibration is raising, there will be others who will be attracted to you because of the *feeling* – of the vibrational level that is in you and around you. So we must say to you, "Get more into awareness."

The Burden of Awareness

Silver Bough 2:4: "Go gather the sincere seekers and deliver them from the delusions generated in dense bodies."

—*The Kolbrin Bible*

Marshall Masters: Awareness is a heavy burden, so when we first become aware of what is to be; we question our own judgment, as it is unwise to be hasty about dark prospects. In the fullness of time, we gather enough evidence to know that our awareness is not a delusion or some passing fright, but rather, that it is a true and sobering awakening to a dark future. One we will survive, though it will take many of us in the process. Then, in the second heartbeat of this dreadful realization, we are overpowered by our commitments to those we love.

Our first impulse is to share the warning as one would shout fire in a burning building, but this building is not burning quite yet. Not even the smoke from this future fire has fully evidenced itself, so to shout fire when others cannot accept even the faintest smell, is to invite trouble upon ourselves. With a dark certainty of this magnitude, we each must see or smell the smoke for ourselves, before we're willing to pay serious heed to the warnings of others.

This is why awareness is a personal experience and so each of us comes to it in our own unique way. Until everyone sees or smells the danger of fire, you must work quietly to protect them, through self-sacrifice.

Rather than force a message upon them that they are not pre-pared to hear, go quietly about them to make sure the exits are free and open, so when the time comes, there is nothing to hinder their escape. Yes, this is a lonely responsibility but you must be wise enough to understand that standing in your knowing is only meaningful, when you're willing to stand-alone.

In the times ahead, it will be easier to find those of a like mind, who like you are aware and willing to stand in their know-ing alone. Seek them out, if you cannot bear the loneliness, for it is not required that you stand-alone in your knowing.

In the next teaching, the Elohim will explain the importance of preparedness.

Part 4

—

Preparedness and Intuition

There sometimes comes a knock at the door and if we open it unprepared, what steps across the threshold can be a horror we've never seen before. Yet preparing for the unknown is far more difficult than preparing for that which we already know and understand. Sadly, the years ahead will present us with many such doors to open, and behind them will be new realities of danger and woe. Therefore, our best defense is to weave the knowledge of preparedness, with a supreme confidence in our own sense of intuition.

The Cataclysm

Manuscripts 6:24: "Their multitude moved in the gloom of a half dawn, leaving the shattered cities behind them."

—*The Kolbrin Bible*

Marshall Masters: The human mind is a vehicle to the many dimensions spoken of earlier. As multidimensional beings, we must prepare for what is to come, in more dimensions than the physical alone. We must prepare in the spiritual, the mental and the philosophical levels as well for the coming global cataclysm. This is the only practical way to prepare for what is to come, for it will require preparedness on each of these levels to ensure your own survival, and that of those whom you hold dear.

Those who come late to awareness have little time to prepare themselves adequately, if at all. To them, the future events will unfold upon this world as a curse that is happening to them. Consequently, their first impulse will be to separate themselves from its harmful effects.

Yet what they will fail to understand is that there is no place to hide from this horrific future, for it will happen to one and all and in many different ways. The final tally of those who survive and the suffering of those who fall, will mostly be a matter of fortune or misfortune, but not entirely. What the event does to each of us will largely depend on how soon we begin to see ourselves as being a part of it.

When we become a part of it, like the thread of life in the flag we discussed earlier, we begin to feel its movements.

As you listen to this teaching of the Elohim, visualize yourself as a thread of life, and feel the force of nature about you, and that to which you are connected. In simple terms: be the flag.

Preparedness and Intuition

The Elohim: The next thing we wish to speak to you about today is preparedness. You know, we go along our day, and we prepare our food, we prepare our homes, we prepare ourselves for the day. But it goes beyond that.

Preparedness means to be aware, and we spoke to you of that in the first part of this. All of these things that we speak to you of *are* intricately intertwined. There's nothing here that is going to be separate from another.

So, preparedness is all about being prepared. As you prepare for your day, you must prepare for the days ahead. All of you that are listening to this are very aware of the changes that are going on on the Earth at this time. The violent actions of Mother Nature, the violent actions of each other, the — almost surreal thought processes coming forward from people that are in our governments and higher officials.

All of this has become almost commonplace, but yet there are many of you out there that weren't prepared for this. Had you have been aware, you would have been prepared for the times we live in now. So what we suggest to you is to be prepared for the times coming ahead, so that all of this will not become surreal, but will become part of what you know, part of what you are.

Now, this brings into another question of whether the *changes* coming forward on this Earth are destined or prophesied. And as our levels of awareness increase individually, and therefore, exponentially across the world, it can prevent it from being *as* cataclysmic as it will be. However, we will tell you is that the changes will happen, but to what degree or intensity really is dependent upon the humans here on this Earth, and we use that term, humans, in a manner in which just to describe the beings that you all are aware of that are on the Earth plane, because that is another discussion yet, of the different peoples who live among you, species, shall we say. So being prepared, and being prepared for the changes, the world view, the energy levels, the climate changes, the activity in the weather, as well as what's going on around the world.

Many of you who are listening to this are born and bred in the United States, and we would tell you is that being prepared means being prepared worldwide. For other cultures, other countries have very different viewpoints as to what is going on in the world, but it still is going to be the same inasmuch as the changes that are coming forward.

You have to be prepared in your own small communities of where would you go, should there be a disaster or catastrophe. What would you take with you? What would be important for you? I want each and every one of you to look around your home, for this material world is an illusion. You will not take these things with you. These things will become not important; right now, they are a part of your world, because that is the world, in which the illusion has been created, that you are interacting with. But I tell you, you do not need to take these things with you.

You need to learn how to get into your own guidance and to listen to your own guidance, which again brings us back to the awareness, which brings us to the next one that we *will* be talking about, is the knowledge on how to get the awareness and how to prepare yourself. You must prepare your families, and that means your family members. Please understand that not everyone is going to feel the same. They're not going to feel the way you feel, and you have to learn to come to accept that, and you have to learn to be able to deal with that. That comes through your awareness. That's part of being prepared. So we would tell you as you look around your home, if you had to leave your home today, what would you take with you? What would be dependent upon your survival?

We will talk more about the survival mode because it should not be anything to be feared. It is no different than being prepared for going to work each day, to do your homework each day, to get your clothes ready to wear each day, to make your breakfast, lunch or dinner. It is just where are you being prepared at? What is it that you're focusing on?

Intuiting Danger

Manuscripts 6:2: "The leaders of the slaves foretold great events of which the temple seers were not informed."

—*The Kolbrin Bible*

Marshall Masters: We are not only multidimensional beings with multidimensional minds; we are also gifted with brains that can grow with wisdom.

We can actually compare the neural pathways of our minds to the many interwoven threads of a flag, but then, there is even more. Our neural pathways expand and reorganize themselves in direct response to our thoughts, as we transform awareness into preparedness.

One could say this process is similar to programming a modern computer, but this natural process of contemplation yields far more sophisticated results, because it only requires the simple act of contemplation.

This is because the very act of contemplating awareness translates into preparedness. We literally direct our minds to weave new pathways as though it were a magical flag that can sew itself to into even greater purposes. Through such contemplation, we can sew the pathways of our survival within the physical structure of our brains.

When the day comes that we are confronted with the anger of nature, then something marvelous can happen. We will become a part of it and understand it more quickly and more intuitively. This unique ability creates time. Time to get out of the way. Time to move to safety. Time to live another day.

But stepping aside from danger will not be your greatest challenge, for in the coming global cataclysm, you will bear witness to a great suffering. One that will strip away your sense of self and whatever hopes you cherish for the future — if you let it.

There is only one defense for this suffering, and that is knowledge. In the next teaching this series; the Elohim share with us the importance of knowledge in the survival sense.

Part 5

—

Knowledge and Meaning

A small step beyond preparedness is where meaning awaits knowledge. In a survival sense, meaning is the opportunity to remember what works, as well as the dangers lurking in the shadows. Meaning is therefore wisdom codified into folklore that can be easily understood and remembered by even the youngest amongst us. The ancients have thusly used the art of folklore, and it has served them well. In the tribulations ahead, the new meanings we gain, shall become our own gifts of folklore to future generations. Rich with stories of courage and compassion, it too will be imbued with humanity's noblest traditions.

Knowledge is Strength

Wisdom 1:28: "Skill and knowledge are a sword and shield in times of adversity and uncertainty."

— *The Kolbrin Bible*

Marshall Masters: We tend to think of survival in terms of what is in our bunker, our storm shelter, the pantries in our kitchens, and in the haversacks we sling over our shoulders. These are important to be sure, but to survive lengthy trials, once must also know how to feed the soul. A full stomach with a weak spirit is not the way to insure your survival over a period of months and years. Long after the haversack is empty, the pantry bare and the bunkers stripped clean the strength in your soul will be all that remains.

This is why knowledge is as important as food, because while a day without food is a discomfort, a day without hope invites disaster. Herein is the true benefit of knowledge. It is inexhaustible. Once acquired, it nourishes the soul, regardless of whatever is at hand to nourish the body.

This is why knowledge is so vitally important. It gives us the strength and hope to go one step beyond hopelessness, because it reassures us that the dark days will eventually pass. It likewise gives us the confidence to know that one day, we will arise from the ashes of a devastated world, to embrace the sunlight of a new future.

It will be there for those who endure to see it and for those born into it, without knowing the full price paid. Yet they will appreciate those who sought this knowledge for all life to come.

Knowledge and Meaning

The Elohim: As we spoke to you in the other two segments – awareness, preparedness and knowledge – there is no separation between them. They're just simply different aspects of the process that each and every one of you will be going through in the next weeks, months and years to come.

Some people would tell you that knowledge is power, and I would tell you that it's not an accurate statement. Knowledge is simply what it is. It is how it's applied, as to whether it's wise or not. Knowledge comes from not only books, but also from an awareness again, speaking with the guides and being prepared for what they have to tell you. For if you truly stand in your truth, and if you truly wish only to hear the truth, then that comes from being prepared and being aware. And therefore, that comes the knowledge that that which you are receiving from those guides, outside sources, sources inside the self is truth. Because knowledge, as it is applied, is only as good if it *is* applied.

So, as we bring you through, we understand that what we've spoken to you about today in these three segments may not seem very deep. They may not seem very – totally informative, and we recognize that. For what these are is steps. We're going to bring to you, in each of these three areas, as well as continue the growth process by bringing other topics. We will be bringing them into more and more depth, more and more finite details, so that as time goes along, you will be able to start seeing a clear picture. It will be building much like making a cake, and making the many layers, the cake, and then the icing, and the cake, and then the icing. We will be building a grand cake, by the way, all of us together.

For those of you who are here, listening, by sending the energy that you wish to know more, that you wish to really find out what the key is to you, not to your neighbor, not to your spouse, not to your loved one, but to you, then it means about listening, it means about sharing, and it means about intent.

Knowledge that you all have here, on this Earth plane, that are written in your pages, and there's many pages of many books that would tell you this is truth and that is truth. Many of you out there would believe those things that are written within the pages of these books, and we would tell you, we would like for you *now,* when you go and read something, is to *feel* how those words seem to you that are printed on that paper. We'd like for you to feel it because if it doesn't feel right to you, then it is not your truth. That's how you come into knowledge.

We would like to invite you to read or to listen to something, and we would like for you to become aware of how you *feel* about those words that you hear or that you read. If you get nothing from it at all, we would tell you to take that one step further and see if you have a block or obstacle. If you're not sure, that is a good starting point for you, is to start by figuring out how come you did not sense or feel anything one way or another. You may discover that it has nothing to do with you at all, but – you may also discover that you have a block or an obstacle – that you are not aware of that's in place within your being. So we would suggest to you, as you listen to these words and words of others, and as you read books, to make it a point to be aware, because the awareness is what brings preparedness, which brings us to the knowledge of knowing what your truth is. For only you – have the key – to your own truth.

As time goes on, we will expound on this in great depth, about why it is that many of us do not feel the same way about any given material. We will discover what that means in the times ahead.

Why? Why? Why?

Manuscripts 6:39: "The captains had gone and the people revolted because of the calamities which had befallen them."

—*The Kolbrin Bible*

Marshall Masters: When a cataclysmic event happens the first instinct is to act, or to be paralyzed with inertia. Both responses are the direct result of one's level of awareness and preparedness.

Granted, there are those who succumb despite their awareness and those fortunate enough to survive the event by sheer luck alone. However, it is after the initial event when survivors must come to grips with burden of loss, and fears for the future.

Those who are unprepared and unaware will not fathom the deeper reasons for the event. Overwhelmed by suffering and irreconcilable grief they will attribute it to some mysterious cause. A quirk of nature, the vengeance of a deity, or the failing of a corrupt government.

In these settings, the unprepared will seek out those possessing awareness, preparedness and knowledge for guidance. Not only for physical survival, but also to grasp the meaning of what has happened so they can replace the misplaced anger of mystery with the knowledge of a more noble purpose.

When you accumulate knowledge, you are building a stock-pile of meaning, hope and survival wisdom for the days following the initial event. Days when hopelessness will claim lives just as easily as hunger, fatigue and disease: perhaps, even more so.

Use your knowledge now to find peace within you and it will give you the resolve to accept the burden of these future responsibilities. When the time comes, others less knowledgeable and less prepared, will find hope and meaning in your words. Do it not for them or yourself, but for your greatest responsibility: that being your responsibility to our species, and its future survival.

Finding that future will demand a powerful sense of direction and purpose. This is why the next teaching of The Elohim, shows us how responsibility also serves as our inner compass to the future.

Part 6

—

Responsibility and Courage

Courage is the most important human emotion for our species. It defines the threshold between slavery and freedom, and each of us will have to cross it during the coming tribulation. Those who step forward with the integrity of courage will embark upon a journey of freedom. Those who step back in fear will stumble into the abyss of slavery. Yes, humanity has stood here before, but this time is different. We'll either step forward to continue our transformation into a more enlightened species, or we'll collectively commit ourselves to a final fate in the abyss. This is why the guides are lighting the path for us with these teachings. They believe in us.

Your Inner Compass

Silver Bough 3:1: "Good always leads to good and bad always to bad."

—*The Kolbrin Bible*

Marshall Masters: In the confusion and chaos that will surely come in then troubled days ahead, finding our way and leading others to safety becomes a paramount concern. Instinct, more than maps will be the principle guidance mechanism, which is why we must be able to combine all that we have learned in the form of an inner compass. A compass fabricated from awareness, preparedness, knowledge and integrity.

Integrity is the magical force that keeps our inner compass working in the worst of times. Like the magnetic pull of the earth's north pole, it is an unseen, yet powerful force. Without it, the needle swings in any direction it pleases and to whatever urge seems most convenient.

With integrity comes great responsibility for there is never a point at which you can afford to stop learning. Nor can you delay action because you feel as though you haven't learned enough.

In this teaching, the Elohim gather tougher all the thoughts and ideas discussed so far and show you how they can become the functional parts of your own inner compass. One that can and will, lead you through the difficult years ahead with a compassionate wisdom as it guides you to a brighter future.

Responsibility
and Courage

The Elohim: Today, we will continue our conversation on the term, awareness.

Having awareness means taking responsibility. Having awareness – means to do a healing. It means healing in general, and we shall be speaking of that more fully in a moment.

We also spoke to you last time of help and assistance with becoming even more deeply aware, and today we shall also – speak to you more in depth on that.

We will begin with the responsibility of awareness.

There are still many of you that we shall term "lightworkers" that have the awareness of the change, of the ascension, of the vibrational shifts that are upon us, and strengthening even more as the times ahead quickly move forward towards us. We would tell you now is not the time for you to sit back and do nothing.

Now is the time for you to stand up and to share what you know. Many of you think you do not know enough to communicate with others, and we say to you, "Oh, but you do." You must. You – must – communicate, and we understand not all will be in agreement. That is not what matters. What matters is that you begin the process of doing, of taking responsibility for your knowingness by sharing, for we are in the process of creating a grand, new world, and we cannot do that by being hesitant. The responsibility lies upon you each, as individuals.

We spoke to you last time of how to create some of the awareness on a deeper level. We spoke to you of much help and assistance, so we will begin by advising those of you who have not, or do not, meditate, to make this a daily ritual, a daily practice.

Every single day, learn to become attuned with the energy shift around you. It can be as simple as feeling the change with weather patterns as they enter into your geographic area. Understanding when barometric pressures change, when – fronts move in and move out, the feeling of rain before it gets here. Let your body become physically and consciously aware of those changes. Feeling the grass underneath your feet is being aware, but a deeper level of awareness would be to understand and to feel and sense the grass alive under your feet and its root system, as it is routed into Mother Earth. To walk to a tree and hear its story clearly and succinctly, that is a deeper level of awareness. You may get there by deep-level meditation.

Then, we will go to the next aspect of this, which is our healing aspect, which is all part of the awareness.

When we say "healing," we do not envision you as broken or needing to be fixed. We envision it as you becoming more than what you are. Living in this third-dimensional reality, as a human being has worn heavily on many of you who are listening. Its trials, its tribulations, all of those socio-political, environmentally-programmed issues, challenges, negativities that have been with you since you incarnated here on this Earth plane. They still are there. There will be no room for those kinds of restrictions as we continue with these Earth changes and beyond 2012.

So when we speak to you of healing, we use it as a general term to let go of those things, of those programs, of your environment, of what you *think* is truth. Stand in neutrality, let go of the programming. When you do, your world will become clear. You will see things very differently, from a very different perspective. It will be much clearer, less cluttered, and it will resonate with you. For once you do this work, you will be better prepared, going into and beyond 2012.

So – as – a – general recap for today's visit with you, aware-ness – taking responsibility – getting the help and assistance for deep meditation – daily in your ritual. And do the healing work on yourself and on others by letting go of that, which has been restrictive for each and every one of you.

Get up now, and take responsibility. For we need you; you need each other. We are all as one.

Until we meet again.

Holding the Rose

Morals and Precepts 6:2: "Consider the Real Man, the man who reaches out towards godlikeness. He is the man, in whom God has succeeded."

—*The Kolbrin Bible*

Marshall Masters: We often dwell upon our imperfections to a point of inertia; however, we are nonetheless a magnificent species capable of much wisdom, love and spiritual attainment. Many view themselves as being unworthy of the potential; one given to us by the creator. However, a courageous few do possess the courage to achieve it and that is good.

In this great cataclysm to come, those who think of themselves as flawed and imperfect will possess all the excuses they need, to lay down their lives. In doing so, they will serve a purpose that in those days will become self-evident.

Those who cherish the inner potential of our species will have no need for such excuses. Like careful gardeners, they'll nurse the rose of humanity through desperate times, and live to witness it blossom to its full potential.

Yet, every rose has its thorns, so do we cast it aside because it pricks our fingers, or do we handle it gently as we revel in its natural beauty? As you consider this question, remember that the creator designed the rose, with all of its thorny imperfections. Not through judgment, but with love.

We too, were created in the same manner as the humble rose and what makes us grow is not the judgment of others, but the light and love of our creator. Our imperfections and perfections too: All there by the hand of the creator and to a wisdom we will fully understand and appreciate in the light of a new world. It will be an evolved reality, where we have shed our thorns once and for all.

Therefore, the sting we feel today when we embrace loved ones with prospect of this future reality is indeed, a thorny experience: one that tasks any light worker's integrity.

In then next teaching, we will come to understand how integrity helps keep us grounded and safe, when the chaotic emotions of others begin to swirl about us.

Part 7

—

Integrity and
Self-Love

Loving yourself is not about pampering yourself
with adornments, pleasures, fame and the
vacuous admirations of others. It is about
challenging all that you think and feel, each and
every day of your life. This is because; to grow
through enlightenment is the purest form of self-
love. There are others, but in this existence, rising
to meet our own personal challenges with
integrity and love is how we love ourselves best.

Covenants and Contracts

Lucius 13:9: "The good deeds of men are simplicity, austerity, generosity and integrity."

—The Kolbrin Bible

Marshall Masters: In a survival sense, integrity is the magic that makes our inner compass work and work it must, if we are to endure future travails.

Modern societies often use pragmatic concepts such as covenants and contracts to give a working meaning to the term integrity. With this in mind, we will use these pragmatic concepts as our point of reference.

In simple terms, a covenant is a pledge. Something you say you will do without expecting something in return from someone else. You could say that a covenant is essentially an unconditional promise, such as when two people pledge their undying love to each other.

A contract on the other hand, is something you promise with an expectation of return. Ergo, contracts are conditional which explains why they rely on pragmatic language, such as caveat emptor – "buyer beware." Or in other words, read the fine print before you sign on the dotted line.

To make these two pragmatic concepts work, we keep them separate from each other as much as is humanly possible, but happens when they do collide? Well, imagine that someone has given you a covenant of his or her undying love, and then asks you to sign a one-sided prenuptial contract. Is this true love? Not really.

This is because true love is unconditional. Simply put, it is what we do for others with integrity, and without expectation of return. Even so, there is a cosmic return that transcends any material expectation because integrity is the ultimate expression of self-love. This is why it flows within us, like a perpetual wellspring of psychological and spiritual stamina.

A harmonious balance of true love and integrity attracts the loyalties of others within small survival communities. In these pressed circumstances, justice will be swift because your deeds will judge you, and there will be no lengthy appeals. This is because others will quickly see your integrity, or lack of it, and they will not be dissuaded. They will trust your wisdom, and know that your word is your bond – or not.

This is why these teachings of the Elohim are so vital for in 2012, when love and integrity will be the very stuff of survival itself.

Integrity and Self-Love

The Elohim: Welcome. We are the Elohim. Today, we will talk to you of integrity, truth and responsibility.

Integrity is a word to describe an individual's character, as how they operate, not only with themselves, but with others in the workplace, their family, their friends. We would say to each and every one of you who are listening to this to check where you stand on integrity. Are you operating out of integrity, or are you looking for a return on your action? Or if you are looking for a return, a benefit, a pleasure on an action or a deed, then you are not in integrity.

We speak to you of truth. Truth is an objective, and can be a subjective term to each of you who are listening to this. If you have a knowing, which is not the same as belief or faith, but if you have a true knowing of who – you – are, and what – your – purpose – is, and you do not sway from that, even amidst opposition, dissension, or even those who do not think in the same way that you do, and you stand within that moment, that means you are standing in your truth.

Standing in truth and integrity is the job of each and every one of you in the times forthcoming. For, as the times get more chaotic, more confusing, more violent, more upsetting, there will be many who will tell you what the truth is. They are not in integrity, for they have an agenda, which in some cases can be fear, and in other cases can be very cold, manipulative and deceptive by purpose.

There comes a responsibility that each and every one of you must take to yourself. And that is to check if you are in integrity. Check if you are standing in your truth, and let it sway you not. Others' opinions, actions, that they may take upon you, whether it be physical or verbal. For when the time comes, you must be in your place of knowing, which is your truth. And stand – in – the integrity.

We thank you.

The Price of Dishonesty

Morals and Precepts 42:2:
"Lies and deceit are the merchandise of the weakling and coward."

—*The Kolbrin Bible*

Marshall Masters: In the difficult years ahead, love will be the unconditional acts we do to help others and integrity will be the private measure of our own self-love. There will be no fine print, lengthy contracts, or midnight deals struck behind closed doors. None of this shall matter when there is no time for human foolishness: only the time for that which works to the betterment of all.

If you say I love myself, then examine your integrity. Look hard enough so it can stare back at you, and then you will know it for what it is. Understand your own integrity and you will know if you are expressing unconditional love for others as a true person.

Be a true person and you will be dearly loved. Be otherwise, and others will quickly marginalize you. Should that be your fate, you may wake up one day to find yourself all alone, with nothing but your lack of integrity to keep you company. This will be the cost of dishonesty in 2012, and the years beyond.

In then next teaching, we will come to understand the true relationship between love and fear.

Part 8

—

Fear and Love

What we fear is of our own making, for the universe is what it is. To navigate it properly, fear must be understood as a passing impulse, but not the proper one by which to set a course through troubled times. For this we use love, the most powerful force in the universe and beyond. It is so powerful that it brings worlds and galaxies into being. On a human scale, it illuminates our journeys with safety, so do not who allow yourself to become impaled upon your own fears. Rather, navigate around them with the power of love.

The Two Paths

Lucius 13:14: "The lifeforce diversifies into many expressions, the greatest of which is love."

—*The Kolbrin Bible*

Marshall Masters: Love and fear, are the only two absolute emotions. All other human emotions are a shaded variant of one or the other. Each choice we make reflects one of these, and sends us in one of two different directions: towards love or towards fear.

Fear is the easier path. It leads us towards a deceptive darkness: one that beckons with righteous indecision and the promise of wishful outcomes.

Conversely, the path of Love leads us away from fear, towards the light of the creator. This is the more difficult path, because it demands integrity and self-discipline. However, it rewards us with greater strength, sounder wisdom and more often than not, a better outcome.

With every new decision, ask yourself, am I moving towards the darkness of fear because I lack self-discipline and integrity? Or, am I moving towards the path of love and the light of the creator?

Either way, you must know there are no absolutes. No guarantees. No written assurances. Just choices, and the first one is always a matter of direction. The one that leads to the darkness of fear, or the one that leads to the love and light of the creator.

Fear and Love

The Elohim: Welcome. We are the Elohim, and today, we will speak to you of fear and of love. These are the two most primordial emotions that a human carries within them.

Fear is a term that has been misconstrued. Love is a term that is misunderstood.

When a person thinks of the term, fear, most generally speaking, they think of something, which frightens them, scares them, causing the adrenaline to flow.

When most people think of love, they think of love as that which we have for a mother, a father, a child, a friend or a mate.

These two emotions are all there is. There is no more. There is either fear, or there is love. Fear is an emotion that causes deception and greed and ego. It lacks trust, ambition, and motivation. It cares not about truth. Love is the ultimate goal, for once a person experiences the *true* emotion of love from the Creator, everything else will seem insignificant to that moment of Nirvana.

But from the emotion of love comes compassion and honesty and sharing and mercy. We can express love in gentler ways, helping an individual who is disabled, taking care of a stray cat or dog that has wandered upon your place. Caring for, nurturing; those are all aspects of love.

When we speak of fear and we speak of love, we ask each of you, as individuals, to look inside of yourself, and look at how you process your day. Are you acting or reacting out of a fear-based mechanism, or are you acting or reacting from a love basis?

The soul's purpose here is to experience both fear and love. Ultimately, it is a choice, for the times ahead are going to be more than challenging. We would say to you that those that still are acting or reacting out of fear, your time will be more difficult. You will not see things with clarity, if you are in a fear mode. We would ask that you simply look.

For those of you who are striving to be processing and interacting from the basis of love, we would say to you there's still much work that you need to do.

Please try to strengthen all the aspects of love that you can for the times ahead, for you are all loved by the Creator.

The Death of Ego

Silver Bough 6:27 "Weak men are carried away by their own arrogance and conceit."

—*The Kolbrin Bible*

Marshall Masters: Always remember this: fear is the knife's edge of death. Follow fear and you'll inevitably stumble upon a knife. Also know that ego is a fear-based reflection of your base instincts. Greed, envy lust and so forth. There is nothing inspirational about ego; other than it can brand you as being — egotistical: a less than noble way to be thought of by others.

In 2012, ego will have serious downsides, far beyond the human vanities of today. Likewise, the institutions … various ologies and … various isms that drive our sense of position and stability will be no less vulnerable to cataclysm, than our own fragile egos.

When dark clouds gather, many will scramble to save crumbling institutions and belief systems. Those that exist at the sufferance of ego, no matter how cherished they may be, will suffer the same fate as the egos they breed. Brittle and inelastic, they are easily swept aside by the winds of change and new realities.

Then to our dismay they shatter, no differently than glass figurines crashing down upon a cold marble floor.

In 2012, love, not ego, will give us the spiritual shoes to walk over the broken remains of ego-driven institutions and beliefs. In this regard, unconditional love, like a sturdy pair of boots, will give you ample protection and comfort.

Conversely, ego is as thin as paper and like paper, and so it affords little protection. This is why those experiencing the death of ego are left with a paper-thin separation between them and the carnage about them. A sudden separation from the world about them, that will invariably leave them paralyzed with fear.

As difficult as this may sound, leave those stricken by the death of ego to their own fate. They've made their choices and you've made yours. Like drowning people, they can drag you down with them, and most likely will. In the years to come; the daily decisions of life and death will shape a new reality. Choose unwisely and fate may be unkind. On the other hand, choose wisely and you will certainly live to choose again.

Also know this: the baggage of your own attachments can affect you choices and sometimes, in the most unfortunate ways. In the next teaching in this series, The Elohim explain how to use the liberating power of detachment for more positive outcomes.

Part 9

—

Detachment and Loss

Do we truly lose others, when all of us have existed in one form or another since the beginning of time? Or do we lose each other at the end of time itself? These questions haunt us, but the answer is simple. There is no end to it, just new beginnings and new futures to explore together. No two are alike and the future we are about to enter shall challenge us with a turbulent passage, but it also heralds something more important than surviving cataclysm alone. A better future just beyond the horizon of our furthest dreams and to reach it, we must endure this transit with courage, accept its brevities with grace, and share its meager gifts with compassion. Never forget. It shall pass.

Surviving in the Moment

Wisdom 2:11: "A man is paid according to his labour, and idle hands make a hungry mouth."

—*The Kolbrin Bible*

Marshall Masters: In our everyday lives we are attached to things, such as shiny red sports cars. We spend great sums of money for them and all of the attended duties of ownership. This we happily do for a few thrilling hours of excitement behind the wheel.

When life is good, we can easily afford the things we do to keep our shiny new sports cars racing down the road and willingly so: even gladly so, simply because we can.

In the cataclysmic years ahead our shiny red sports cars will become abandoned wrecks scattered alongside mostly impassable roadways. Then our attention will turn from driving shiny read sports cars, to the more mundane need for shiny cans of stewed red tomatoes. Or whatever else will ease our hunger in the night.

This may sound odd now, but in the days to come, finding a dusty can of stewed red tomatoes will be more thrilling than the memory of driving a sports car. That is, if we can forget our attachments to them and all the other useless clutter of our present-day material lives.

Herein is an issue of vital importance to all those who wish to survive the coming cataclysm. Daydream about your sports cars and the other clutter of your past, and you'll be too preoccupied to notice those half-buried cans of stewed red tomatoes. In the future, a sense of detachment will help nourish both your stomach and your soul.

Detachment and Loss

The Elohim: Welcome. We are the Elohim, and we will be speaking of you in a different manner today, of your fellow man, of your family, of your friends and your co-workers. We will be speaking to you today of detachment.

It is not *truly* an opposite of attachment, but for us to explain detachment, we have to explain the process of attachment.

Many of us get attached to material objects, such as a car, a house, a ring, a painting or all of the material things around you, we become attached to those. It becomes part of our identity. It becomes such an integral part of who we view ourselves as that we lose ourselves in that attachment.

We can attach ourselves to outcomes, as well; family dramas, dramas at work, negative scenarios between people. We become attached to the outcome. We become attached to a success or failure ratio. We would tell you, we will – tell you in this moment that success is never measured by the outcome, but rather by the steps taken, the action, if you will.

When we look at attachments, we attach ourselves emotionally, mentally, sometimes physically, to people, to places, to things, to emotions. They become our source, again, of identity.

We would tell you how important it is to detach yourself from that bondage of outcome, of control and manipulation, of a scene, a scenario, a family issue or process. When you can begin to move through your day without attachment to your home, to your car, to your boss's mood, to the price of milk, you will effectively free yourself from that which binds you to a lower vibration.

Some of you who are listening to this will say, "That means to give up one's emotions," and we would simply say to you, "That is not true." To have no attachment to an outcome means that you are simply letting it unfold without becoming a part of it, without an investment, so to speak.

So detaching yourself from the whole premise that there has to be an outcome that you can perceive has to be let go. For when you let go and become detached is when you can truly experience the emotions that are uniquely designed for the human experience.

We know for many of you listening that this may be somewhat difficult to follow, but we would simply ask that you let these words resonate within you and try to test your own ability to let go of something. Choose one thing for every day that *you are not going to attach* an outcome to, and you will know how freeing and liberating it is to the soul and the spirit.

We thank you.

The Long Goodbye

Britain 4:12: "So let us not
disagree, but take something
of value to all."

—*The Kolbrin Bible*

Marshall Masters: What do you when those you love, refuse awareness? What *do* — you do? After all, the very thought of losing someone you love is excruciating, because such losses create a permanent emptiness in our life: and they can never be refilled quite the same way. Consequently, when we come to awareness and gaze into the future, what do we feel? We first feel the fear of losing those dear to us and so we raise the alarm to warn them.

Yet, when we warn those who are not aware, we tend to become a thorn in their sides. Why do such noble sentiments fail us? It is because awareness is always buried just beyond the thorn's reach. Therefore, to press the issue against those you hold dear, will only frighten and anger them, and no good can come of this.

Always remember that awareness is a personal possession, one that can only be set free by those who possess it. You cannot free that which you do not possess. This is why you must respect their lack of awareness, as painful as that may be. In difficult circumstances such as these you must stand back, so that you can stand in your knowing and hold it privately unto yourself. Why is this necessary?

Not all of us are destined to see the years beyond 2012. Each of us made our own covenant with the creator before we incarnated, to make it to, through or beyond the coming global cataclysm. This is why each of us becomes aware at different times and in different ways.

This is also why it is imperative to respect the awareness of others, as well as their self-imposed lack of it. Focus instead on your own preparation so that you can help them, when the time comes, if it is to come. If not, respect their covenant with the creator, no matter how much pain it will cause you.

Do this now and begin to enjoy their company each day. Cherish each moment as though it were a beautiful desert flowering after a summer rain. Momentarily vibrant in our senses, we know it wither away to be reborn, but for the day, it is ours to enjoy.

This is called the long goodbye and it is your quiet burden. To love and enjoy the company of those you hold dear while respecting their right to free the awareness within them, in a time and a manner of their own choosing. If they choose not to set it free, that too is their rightful choice. If a loved one's 2012 destiny follows a shorter path than your own, then yours is the longer covenant with the creator. That is all there is to it.

When they do pass from you, the loss of a long goodbye will be endurable. Without it, the loss will be a sudden and the grief it creates will diminish your ability to carry on for yourself and those who depend upon you.

If your covenant with the creator leads you on a longer path, begin saying your long goodbyes now, but only if you must. As you do, gather precious moments as loving memories with the greatest of care, for they will comfort you in the lonely nights to come. Awareness is a choice and the long goodbye is a way to honor their covenants, and yours as well.

In the next teaching in this series, the Elohim will explain the nature of duality and how to use it for survival.

Part 10

—

Duality and
The Sexes

The only hope for humanity is that we survive together as co-equals: both men and women, regardless of race, color, creed or position. This is because there are no preordained positions of infallible superiority in the cosmos, nor are there inescapable positions of subservience. Rather, all are connected, co-equally. However, when we allow adversity or greed to polarize us, we begin to lose the very cosmic connections woven into us by our creator, to ensure our future survival as a species. If 2012 teaches us anything; it shall be that we are better than that.

Judgment Clouds Duality

Sons of Fire 5:116 "My judgment will be bent towards a benefit rather than a loss."

—*The Kolbrin Bible*

Marshall Masters: Duality in a future survival sense is a straightforward concept. However, our present day world view often defines it in subjective terms, such as believer and non-believer. Consequently, the more we use judgment to subjectively distinguish these dualities, the more indistinguishable they become. Even for theologians, philosophers and other moralists.

Granted, we can tolerate this subjective brain candy in a comfortable world, but not when we're trying to survive a global cataclysm. This is because clouding our perceptions of duality with subjective judgment is self-defeating and dangerous.

Imagine that you're standing before a mirror. If you judge yourself to be a good person, this is the reflection you'll expect to see in the mirror. If you are a bad person, you'll see the same reflection, unless you've honestly judged yourself first. Either way, how can you subjectively know for certain that the reflection in the mirror is you, as opposed to someone else?

As you listen to The Elohim explain duality, search inward to know if you are ready to free yourself of judgment as the answer will have a direct bearing on your ability to navigate the troubled years ahead, with greater safety.

Duality and The Sexes

The Elohim: Welcome. Today, we will speak to you of duality. It has been a term that has caused quite a struggle for humanity. For when one talks about the Creator, they do not talk about the Creator as a dual entity, but rather as a singular entity. Yet, we live in a world, by its very construct, is dual in nature. Male – female, night – day, good – bad, these are all examples of the term duality.

So how does a human being continue its growth with the duality in its very nature, yet comes from a singular source known as the Creator? When we look at duality, we would tell you that it is simply the balance, and it is the nature of the construction of this planet. But it, too, is an illusion. It is part of the process, if you will, of the soul or spirit to recognize that there *is* no such thing as good – or bad, right – or wrong, male – or female, but we simply coexist with those aspects of the duality.

It is the dynamics of the process of going through this duality construction that *may* – assist those in the years to come, for understanding that it is an illusion will help you to see beyond the events taking place as either good or bad, or that one side is good, and the other is evil, or that one choice is bad, or another is good. For up until this point, we have given you many things along the way, to assist you in the process, to compensate, shall we say, for the duality of your existence.

When we conclude our series, we shall pull all of these things into one place for you, to make sense out of this process that you are all going through in the days, the weeks, months and years ahead.

2012 is fast approaching, and the events are cataclysmic, they're incomprehensible, and they are misunderstood. So by working with these lessons will give you yet a better, a deeper, more profound understanding of your individual purpose, as well as humanity's purpose in the weeks, months and years ahead.

We thank you.

Men and Women

Wisdom 6:3: "Always treat a woman with reserve and respect, for by doing so, you enhance your own standing as a man."

—*The Kolbrin Bible*

Marshall Masters: In 2012 and beyond, the most critical duality for our species will be that of man and woman, and this duality gives rise to a troubling question. How can we as a species survive a global cataclysm and still recognize ourselves?

Answering this question was my quest when I set out to write, Godschild Covenant: Return of Nibiru. An action love story set against a backdrop of a human tribulation on such a grand scale as to be nearly unimaginable. It is here; the story of my epiphany begins: one that started before the first page was written and then haunted me from one chapter to the next.

I've long believed men and women to be co-creators and co-equals. Only in our joining, can we make possible the greatest design for our species. Yet, we often abuse this sacred duality with callous disregard for the greater good, much the same way we fail ourselves as the stewards of our fragile planet.

And so I wondered if the coming tribulation would push us down a rocky slope of subjugation and disrespect, and in doing so; fail us to a darker world? Or, could we endure as co-creators and co-equals and live on, to build a beautiful new world? As I authored my novel, these two possibilities often visited my thoughts, like a gentle touch on the shoulder.

Committed to resolving this riddle, I explored the duality of our sexes through the relationships between the heroes and heroines in my novel. Through them, I sought clarity and it did come to me, but not until the manuscript was finally ready for the printer.

It was then, I experienced my epiphany: one so simple, yet profound. In that glorious instant, the hundreds of pages I'd written became a minuscule price for admission into the theater of human destiny and evolution.

As I beheld this epiphany for the first time, I wondered if I had accidentally stumbled upon it many pages ago, without even recognizing it. It would be a passing thought of no consequence, for finally, here it was, radiating the warmth of insight, like a morning sun rising majestically above a dark and distant horizon.

Yes, this was my glorious epiphany. Humankind will survive and evolve as an enlightened species, for as long as men and women can love and cherish each other, for their differences. It is this duality of differences that strengthens us all, because it is a duality conceived by our Creator, to match two perfectly different parts.

The dark days facing us shall be difficult, but in this crucible of evolution we will awaken in great numbers to this epiphany and our species will flourish. Nurtured by this enlightened duality, distant generations will come to dwell amongst the stars in vast numbers and they will proudly say: we came out of Earth, and our Earth mothers and Earth fathers loved us.

In the next teaching of this series, the Elohim explain our right to choose, as a responsibility and as a gift.

Part 11

—

The Gift of Choice

Choice is the most precious right of sentience and the creator universally gifts it to all sentient life, whether it is incarnated of this world or another. What makes it so precious is that it enables us as a sentient race to evolve, or devolve, if we so choose. Therefore, it is too precious gift to be squandered on mere baubles or vanity. Rather, honor the creator's gift by considering your choices wisely, and for the greatest good.

Crucible of Evolution

Gleanings 15:32: "There are many roads the soul may travel to self-consciousness."

—*The Kolbrin Bible*

Marshall Masters: As precious as life is, the creator also gives us a responsibility and a gift that is equally precious, if not more so. It is choice: the choice to choose wisely, or unwisely for that matter.

We have a responsibility to learn from unwise choices and when we choose not to, fate makes the final choice for us. This is why choice is the crucible of evolution. It is how we experience our world, each other and our own uneven steps on the pathway of life.

This right is an essential tool in our evolution and when we knowingly allow others to limit it — that is a choice. When we knowingly allow others to deny us the best possible choices — that is a choice too. So regardless of what we choose, knowingly or unknowingly, the consequences inevitably become a permanent fixture in the tapestry of our lives.

Shortsighted and self-interested choices, made at the expense of others, turn into musty fabrics, hanging limply in the dark. Always there, we push them from one side to the other to avoid the flicker of a truthful torch.

There are better choices.

To choose compassion is a better choice. To choose love and caring are better choices too and all these choices, no matter how clumsily we act them out, are born of a noble purpose. The more of these that decorate the tapestry of your life, the richer it will be. When you choose to make a positive difference in the lives of others, you are making a choice inspired by our creator.

Granted, these better choices do not always come naturally, nor do they get easier with practice, but this too is by design. The dark days ahead will usher in burdensome choices: ones that will tax us, each and every day. Be faithful to the creator's purpose and your choices will help to ease your burden. Woven into your heart, they'll brighten the tapestry of your life. Always accessible and nurturing, they will be forever yours.

The Gift of Choice

The Elohim: Today, we shall be speaking to you of a culmination of all things that we have brought forward to you up to this point.

We are going to begin by talking about the healing aspect of the human being, and again, we would ask that you re-frame the term, healing, for you are not broken, you are not ill, and you are not sick.

Healing is a generic term that you have all used for the purpose of identifying to make oneself better. So the purpose of *this* culmination of all the teachings to this point is going to end where we start, which is the healing.

When we speak to you of the soul's journey here on earth. Those of you who are listening must understand that this was a conscious or unconscious, but choice, nonetheless, that you made to experience this time forthcoming. We're specifically going to give you the reference point of 2012.

There has been much speculation, much conversation and much communication, as to the event, itself. It is a celestial event, to be sure. Beyond that, the event, of itself is what will mold humanity to become greater than it is now.

The opportunity exists in the now to create a better place in the years following the celestial event.

Many of you have experienced a sense of loss or grieving, a sense of understanding that your choice to survive or to go forward in 2012 has left you estranged among those that you thought loved you, cared for you, understood you, but that knowingness that you have *is* the truth. You must stand in that integrity, and with that knowingness comes that responsibility. To thyself – to thyself – that is not a selfish thing to be. It is one that comes from strength.

When you are going through these steps of emotional stages, much fear shall come forward. That fear is what you do not need to suppress. What you need to do with that fear is to acknowledge it and then replace it with the opposite emotion.

When we go back to the healing, when a human being stands in their truth and their knowing, there is a vibration that's emitted that's almost tangible by others around them. If you begin your process in earnest today, you will begin emitting this vibration, and with this comes a domino effect, in which others will see you standing in your truth, that you're learning to heal yourself, that you're learning detachment, and they too shall rise above from where they are in their moment.

Survival in Focus

Creation 7:4: True victory is
gained over the defeated
bodies of vanquished pas-
sions and baser selves.

—The Kolbrin Bible

Marshall Masters: Those who choose to peacefully coexist with others, share a world view far different from those who exploit and subjugate others for their own self-interested agendas. To illustrate this difference, let's imagine the self-interested choices of exploitation and subjugation as the mechanical workings of a zoom lens camera.

The more powerful your zoom lens, the further out you can see, but even if you have a weak zoom lens, the same process applies. And this process begins with seeking out targets of opportunity in the blurry world about you. Once you spot something of interest, the next step is to bring it into focus.

The last step in this process, requires fine-tuning with small adjustments until you have a perfectly framed picture of what it is, you want to exploit or subjugate. With that, you take the picture and proceed to the next target of opportunity. All is well and good, that is until a minor glitch develops.

As you scan your blurry world of opportunities, a persistent blur begins to dart in and out, around the edge of your camera's viewfinder. Then after a while, it disappears just as mysteriously as when it first appeared. Curious but beyond practical focus, you choose to ignore it until a more convenient day, and resume searching for easier targets of opportunity.

Then one day, the blur begins popping in and out of your viewfinder again. As you debate whether or not to expend the necessary effort to frame it and focus in on it, it suddenly jumps into focus all on its own, and there it is. What you now see in your viewfinder, is a perfectly framed and focused picture of gnarled teeth, the gnarled teeth of a terrible monster wearing a necklace of broken cameras, and he is smiling hungrily at you. Not a pretty picture.

On the other hand, those who choose to see the world about them through love and service to others, use a natural gift. One given to us by our creator that is so perfect, we have no need for expensive zoom lens cameras to pursue myopic, self-interested agendas.

Rather, we use our natural loving gift to see all about us in perfect detail. Regardless of how near or far a thing may be; all is there. All is in focus and when the monstrous exploiters with their gnarled teeth and broken camera necklaces appear, we easily avoid them. We simply step aside, to let them feast upon the smaller exploiters, for as big fish eat the big fish; big exploiters eat small exploiters as well.

So this is the power of choice given to us by our creator. Use it to live. Use it to survive. Use it as the creator intended, and you will capture images of love and compassion that will forever brighten your soul.

In the next and final teaching in this series, the Elohim share their final thoughts and suggestions for 2012, and the years beyond.

Part 12

—

2012 and Beyond

In all that we say and do, the reality of what lies beyond 2012 is a destiny of choice. We of this Earth as well as The Elohim and countless others share a common destiny. To evolve closer to the creator, by serving each other. These words are neither trite nor hastily spoken, for they offer a powerful truth. It is the greatest hope held for us by all enlightened species. That through love and integrity, humanity will rise above its tribulations and firmly grasp the rung of a higher destiny.

Beacons of Hope

Gleanings 17:9: "Beyond the pains from a sojourn of tears, there shines a glorious rainbow of hope and joy."

—*The Kolbrin Bible*

Marshall Masters: How each of us approaches this coming global cataclysm, reflects our personal covenant to the creator. There are three such convents, and we each pledged one of them before incarnating in this life.

One large portion of us has already chosen to fall at the outset of the cataclysm. Another will fall midway through it, helping others where they can. The smallest portion, shall endure to see the Earth reborn. In the grand scheme of things; each is equally important and equally necessary to our evolution as a species.

Those who made their covenant to fall at the outset shall serve a great purpose. To energize a massive, sudden and profoundly shocking awakening experience for humankind. Then, the old divides and prejudices, which have long separated us, shall melt away as quickly as their lives, and those left standing will begin forging new and necessary fellowships of survival.

Those who fall midway through the cataclysm, will also do so in fulfillment of their covenants to the creator. The end of their lives will not be their sacrifice, but rather, each difficult step they take to that end. With the last measure of their lives, they will help to energize many fellowships of survival and they'll encourage those destined to go beyond, to take another step forward.

This is why the greatest responsibility shall weigh upon those who've made their covenants to endure the dark times, and to help build the world anew. Who are these precious few? To see them now is but to see a past reflection, because the cataclysm will forever change them. They shall become as different to who and what they are now, as night is to day.

Their souls will be tempered in the hot coals of catastrophe and like a Phoenix; they will emerge from the flames as the magnificent seed stock of a new future. They shall be our beacons of hope for a new beginning, and it will be a grand and glorious one. Believe it.

2012 and Beyond

The Elohim: 2012 shall bring such a surreal series of chain reactions of events that you *must* be prepared. You must stand in your truth, you must do your own work, you must help others that have an earnest interest in becoming more than.

You must understand that that feeling of loss that you may experience from those who *do not* understand, they *choose* not to understand. That is where it is so invaluable to learn detachment. For if you get caught in the drama – of others – and their agendas, their path, then you shall not be standing in your truth, in your knowing, in your integrity, and the events that take place will be doubly difficult for you.

We would tell you to find that love, that one that we spoke to you of previously, called Nirvana. If you could only experience that for one – second, you will then have the knowing, you are not alone. It will vibrate through you much like a battery assists a toy to play. We use that analogy for the purpose of joy and lightheartedness, for though this be serious, and this be extraordinarily difficult to absorb, we tell you, you are not alone.

Meditate, contemplate, release the fears, the attachments, stand in your knowing, stand in your truth, recognize that the duality is just an illusion and that you are not separate, for you're not.

We are watching the events as they take place, and we promise you there are others who are watching this event take place. There is much assistance on this Earth plane. Step up your vibrations, communicate, expand, grow and you will help others who are going through the same thing to become more than what they are for the purpose of not only surviving 2012, but creating a brand new, beautiful world here on Earth.

We love you. We are done.

Vision Quest

Gleanings 15:24: "I shall seek the man who is ever seeking to unravel the riddle of life."

—*The Kolbrin Bible*

Marshall Masters: In the first part of this of this program we looked at the various covenants we all make to the creator before we incarnate. To perish in the early days of the cataclysms: or in the midst of them. Those few of us who've made their covenant to live on as beacons of hope will shoulder the greatest responsibility: to nurture the evolution of our species towards a more evolved, enlightened and compassionate future.

Perhaps you have been wondering about your own covenant with the creator. What did you pledge before you incarnated, and will that covenant be your irrevocable fate? Wonder no more for there is good news.

Never forget that the creator has endowed each of us with something precious, if not more precious, than life itself. It is the right to choose. To choose wisely when we can, and should we choose unwisely, to accept responsibility for that outcome, so as to learn from it.

This now brings us to you, and all those hearing my voice at this most precious moment, because I wish to share with you a powerful concept. One that is best understood after receiving all of the other teachings in this series. It is simple, but so important, that if you only remember one thing, please remember this.

Whether you are incarnated or unincarnated makes no difference, because you're no less precious to the creator; it is just where you happen to be in time, and the only constants of time are that it always changes and that we continually change in response to it. This is by design and likewise, you have an equal right to choose a different outcome to your covenant.

If you made your covenant to perish at the outset or midway into this global cataclysm and now wish to go beyond as a beacon of hope for humankind, then do so. It is your right to choose this new outcome. Likewise, if you made your covenant to be a beacon of hope but no longer desire the burden of that responsibility, you can choose to yield your life for the betterment of the species. That too is your right to choose, and this now brings us to the closing thought of this series. Taking your next step.

It is not the way of The Elohim to decide your path for you, but merely to offer their wisdom as one possible starting point, and the spiritual survival concepts they've shared with you have withstood the cosmic test of time.

Use their wisdom in your own way and in your own time, for in the difficult years ahead, the only useful wisdom is that which resonates deeply within your own soul. So deeply, it gives you the strength you need to stand in your knowing, regardless of the tribulations ahead. How do you find it? That's your next step, if you choose.

The ancient ancestors of the various indigenous peoples of our world have survived previous global cataclysms. Through their folklore and traditions, they've passed on the harbingers signs of the next cataclysm to their decedents. Harbinger signs that are now coming to pass, and which give us reason to heed their warnings and sage advice.

An ancient ceremony practiced in one form or another by the various indigenous peoples of the world awakens personal growth. We often refer to these ceremonies as vision quests, and they are very personal experiences. Ones not to be taken lightly for they have helped the indigenous peoples of our world to survive multiple global cataclysms in what is now a very distant and nearly forgotten past.

In simple terms, a vision question is how you find relevant new truths, while casting aside old ones that never really were. Finding who and what is truly relevant to you and your future is a deep personal responsibility. One you must do alone for there is no other way.

Granted, the first step of any vision quest is daunting, but with self-discipline and persistence, progress will nurture your soul in the most magnificent and illuminating ways imaginable. What will the first step of your own vision quest look like? It will look like your choice. Choose well. Choose love. And always choose to go to the light.

This is Marshall Masters for the Elohim and their voice in this series of teachings, Rebecca Jernigan wishing you peace and hope for the days ahead.

Appendices

"Chance favors the
prepared mind."
—*Louis Pasteur*

Appendix A — Complete Quotations from The Kolbrin Bible

Segment	As Used in Video	Unabridged Quote
Part 1 — Our Prophetic Dreams		
Prophetic Dreams and Visions	**Creation 4:3:** "There were some who struggled harder, because their desires were turned Godward, and they were called The Children of God."	**Creation 4:3:** "There were some who struggled harder, were more disciplined; because their forefathers had crossed the great dark void; their desires were turned Godward, and they were called The Children of God."
My Own Prophetic Dream	**Silver Bough 2:12:** "When the implications of my fate awoke knowledge in my heart, I wept, in the spirit-lit darkness."	**Silver Bough 2:12:** "When the implications of my fate awoke knowledge in my heart, I wept, in the spirit-lit darkness, for my wife, for my children; for would they not become fatherless? Who would harness the oxen and scatter the seed over the soil? Who would tend the sheep and stand guard, who would protect from intruders?"
Godschild Covenant Discovery	**Creation 2:23:** "Where is there a wiser father than the Spirit of God, or a better mother than Earth?"	**Creation 2:23:** "Where is there a wiser father than the Spirit of God, or a better mother than Earth? What man is now he owes to these; may he learn to be duly grateful. Above all, let him never forget the lessons learned in his upbringing."

Segment	As Used in Video	Unabridged Quote
Part 2 - We are The Elohim		
Speaking with The Elohim	**Scrolls 16:7:** "This is the secret of life: Man lives in God and God lives in man. This answers all questions."	**Scrolls 16:7:** "This is the secret of life: Man lives in God and God lives in man. This answers all questions."
We are Multi-dimensional Beings	**Scrolls 9:6:** "The clouds obscuring the lesser lights, darken the face of wisdom."	**Scrolls 9:6:** "The clouds obscuring the lesser lights are the clouds of misconception, which darken the face of wisdom."
Part 3 — Survival Awareness		
Be the Flag	**Morals and Precepts 45:11-12:** "A friend is one who silences your opponents when you are not there."	**Morals and Precepts 45:11** "A friend is not one who agrees with your argument; he is not one who frequents your abode; he is not one who sings your praises, nor is he one who converses pleasantly or bears gifts. 12.He is one who encourages you when misfortune presses, who lends his arm when you are down, who walks by your side when men flee from you, and who silences your opponents when you are not there."
The Burden of Awareness	**Silver Bough 2:4:** "Go gather the sincere seekers and deliver them from the delusions generated in dense bodies."	**Silver Bough 2:4:** "Go, gather the sincere seekers, and reveal to them a little light; guide them through the bewitching fairyland of earthly illusion, so they leave it to enter the daylight of Truth and not the darkness of death. Deliver them from the delusions generated in dense bodies."

Segment	As Used in Video	Unabridged Quote
Part 4 — *Preparedness and Intuition*		
The Cataclysm	**Manuscripts 6:24:** "Their multitude moved in the gloom of a half dawn, leaving the shattered cities behind them."	**Manuscripts 6:24:** "The slaves spared by the Destroyer left the accursed land forthwith. Their multitude moved in the gloom of a half dawn, under a mantle of fine swirling grey ash, leaving the burnt fields and shattered cities behind them. Many Egyptians attached themselves to the host, for one who was great led them forth, a priest prince of the inner courtyard."
Intuiting Danger	**Manuscripts 6:2:** "The leaders of the slaves foretold great events of which the temple seers were not informed."	**Manuscripts 6:2:** "The leaders of the slaves, which had built a city to the glory of Thom, stirred up unrest, and no man raised his arm against them. They foretold great events of which the people were ignorant and of which the temple seers were not informed."
Part 5 — *Knowledge and Meaning*		
Knowledge is Strength	**Wisdom 1:28:** "Skill and knowledge are a sword and shield in times of adversity and uncertainty."	**Wisdom 1:28:** "Do not use lewd expressions or foul language, for this advertises your inferiority to others. Do not laugh at sly or dirty humour, for this displays an unclean and unhealthy mind. Do not raise money or possessions to the status of a god. Fit yourself to earn an honest and useful livelihood. Skill and knowledge are jewels in times of prosperity, a sword and shield in times of adversity, and sure guides through times of uncertainty."
Why? Why? Why?	**Manuscripts 6:39:** "The captains had gone and the people revolted because of the calamities which had befallen them."	**Manuscripts 6:39:** "Tidings of the disaster came back by Rageb, son of Thomat, who hastened on ahead of the terrified survivors because of his burning. He brought reports unto the people that the host had been destroyed by blast and deluge. The captains had gone, the strong men had fallen, and none remained to command. Therefore, the people revolted because of the calamities which had befallen them. Cowards slunk from their lairs and came forth boldly to assume the

Segment	As Used in Video	Unabridged Quote
		high offices of the dead. Comely and noble women, their protectors gone, were their prey; of the slaves the greater number had perished before the host of Pharaoh."

Part 6 — Responsibility and Courage

Segment	As Used in Video	Unabridged Quote
Your Inner Compass	**Silver Bough 3:1:** "Good always leads to good and bad always to bad."	**Silver Bough 3:1:** "I am the prophet of the day; now hear my voice. There is a law of compensation; good always leads to good and bad always to bad; whatever the demands made upon you, they are always within reason. To you who defraud the poor and oppress the weak and defenceless, I tell you, your day is coming."
Holding the Rose	**Morals and Precepts 6:2:** "Consider the Real Man, the man who reaches out towards godlikeness. He is the man, in whom God has succeeded."	**Morals and Precepts 6:2:** "Consider the Real Man, the man who reaches out towards godlikeness. He is the man, in whom God has succeeded. He is God's elect. He is like unto a spreading tree planted in black soil, which blossoms quietly and doubles the yield of its fruit in the summer. Its fruit is a delight to the mouth and fills the stomach with satisfaction. Beneath the canopy of its foliage, the weary find a pleasant refuge from the heat. In its shade, all men find peace and contentment."

Part 7 — Integrity and Self-Love

Segment	As Used in Video	Unabridged Quote
Covenants and Contracts	**Lucius 13:9:** "The good deeds of men are simplicity, austerity, generosity and integrity."	**Lucius 13:9:** "Man's prime duty is to himself, and even when he serves others he is serving his own ends; therefore, he should not be hypocritical about his goodness. The good deeds of men are the soulspirit moulders, as also are spirituality, freedom from agnosia, forbearance, love of Truth and justice, tranquillity of heart, simplicity, austerity, generosity and integrity."

Segment	As Used in Video	Unabridged Quote
The Price of Dishonesty	**Morals and Precepts 42:2:** "Lies and deceit are the merchandise of the weakling and coward."	**Morals and Precepts 42:2:** "Lies and deceit are the merchandise of the weakling and coward; avoid contamination from their foul wares by shunning their company. Putrid meat defiles the pure air."

Part 8 — Fear and Love

The Two Paths	**Lucius 13:14:** "The lifeforce diversifies into many expressions, the greatest of which is love."	**Lucius 13:14:** "The lifeforce diversifies into many expressions, the greatest of which is love. This is a prime quality essential to soulspirit awakening, but it may take on many forms. Reverence is a form of love, so is the appreciation of melody and beauty. Uprightness is love manifesting in self-control; wisdom and desire for Truth is another form of love. Duty and obligation call forth an expression of love in a different aspect, though no less strong and beneficial."
The Death of Ego	**SVB:6:27** "Weak men are carried away by their own arrogance and conceit."	**SVB:6:27** "Weak men become drunk with the heady draughts of power and riches; they are carried away by their own arrogance and conceit. They try to turn earthly condition towards serving their own ends and struggle futilely against The Law. Willing slaves of arrogance and selfishness, helpless victims in the stormy seas of rage, lust and violence, these servants of evil hate the divinity within themselves. They hate and fear the small still voice inside. They stifle it; they smother it under the loud clamour of gaiety. They seek solace in strong wine, in sense-stimulating entertainment and in spirit-poisoning drugs. Stand aside; let them be carried swiftly to the place of sorrow and vain regret!"

Part 9 — Detachment and Loss

Surviving in the Moment	**Wisdom 2:11:** "A man is paid according to his labour, and idle hands make a hungry mouth."	**Wisdom 2:11:** "The dispensations of life are not entirely beyond the understanding of man, and indeed he has a duty to strive for understanding. Everything serves a purpose, even things, which seem the most hurtful."

Segment	As Used in Video	Unabridged Quote
		Every ungainly rock has, within itself, a potential statue, and potential beauty lies in every block of wood or lump of clay, but what is there cannot come out of its own volition. The image and the beauty are brought out only after the untouched materials have been subjected to the discipline of thought and the forming action of chisel, knife or fire. According to the good things done by a man, so will he be rewarded, and by the nature of the evil he does, so will he be punished. A man is paid according to his labour, and idle hands make a hungry mouth.
The Long Goodbye	**Britain 4:12:** "So let us not disagree, but take something of value to all."	**Britain 4:12:** "Joseph, our father, said, "I have not come to batter down your house of hope, for it has many pleasing features, even as ours. So let us not disagree, but take the best from both and, discarding what is less good, fashion something of value to all. Let us weigh one thing against the other, rejecting that, which less clearly shows the way."
Part 10 — Duality and The Sexes		
Judgment Clouds Duality	**SOF 5:116:** "My judgment will be bent towards a benefit rather than a loss."	**SOF 5:116:** "A too hasty decision by the judges often inclines towards injustice. Therefore, when the judges have heard all, and every word has been spoken by those who have a right to speak, the judges shall retire and pray. Each should say, within his heart, "I will consider my words carefully before I speak, and they will be uttered in the purity of Truth untainted by falsity or hypocrisy. I will not be harsh in my judgment, and it will be bent towards a benefit rather than a loss. My speech will be directed towards the safeguarding of others and be without any taint of malice or evil intent."

Segment	As Used in Video	Unabridged Quote
Men and Women	**Wisdom 6:3:** "Always treat a woman with reserve and respect, for by doing so, you enhance your own standing as a man."	**Wisdom 6:3:** "Always treat a woman with reserve and respect, for by doing so, you enhance your own standing as a man. It is the men without pride in themselves who hold women in low esteem, and women who submit to such men take a perverted pleasure in their own degradation. When all a man seeks in the company of a woman is frivolity and amusement, he will in the end seek to use her as an instrument of fornication. The wise man keeps well away from the chattering woman, for life with her would be like living at the foot of a sandhill."
Part 11 — The Gift of Choice		
Crucible of Evolution	**Gleanings 15:32:** "There are many roads the soul may travel to self-consciousness."	**Gleanings 15:32:** "If a man follow a false god with goodwill and honesty, serving men well and living in accordance with My laws, I will not repudiate him, and he will not be denied enlightenment on the way. There are many roads along which the soul may travel to bring about its development and awakening to self-consciousness, but is it not advantageous to choose the best one? Only the foolish travel blindly, without seeking guidance and directions. Those who have little wisdom or who are easily misled follow roads which go nowhere. They who follow a barren faith reach a barren destination, they find only an empty place devoid of hope, incapable of fulfilling their dreams and aspirations."
Survival in Focus	**Creation 7:4:** "True victory is gained over the defeated bodies of vanquished passions and baser selves."	**Creation 7:4:** "To this and similar parts of the Otherworld, the wicked would be drawn when they passed through the grim gates of death. But Habaris taught a different conception of wickedness, one where lack of effort, indolence and indifference to duty and obligations, the taking of the easy path, were just as wrong as actual deeds of wickedness. He taught that men reach the true goal of life by transmuting lustlove into

Segment	As Used in Video	Unabridged Quote
		truelove. That true victory is gained only over the defeated bodies of their vanquished passions and baser selves."
Part 12 — 2012 and Beyond		
Beacons of Hope	**Gleanings 17:9:** "Beyond the pains from a sojourn of tears, there shines a glorious rainbow of hope and joy."	**Gleanings 17:9:** "I am the imprisoned captive longing for return to the freedom of the infinite. Yet, because of my mortal love I feel heartpangs of sorrow for things that pass away. But I know that beyond the pains inseparable from a sojourn in the vale of tears, there shines a glorious rainbow of hope and joy. There is a place of abiding love centred on the infinite; there, if you will but cherish me, we shall not be denied expression."
Vision Quest	**Gleanings 15:24:** "I shall seek the man who is ever seeking to unravel the riddle of life."	**Gleanings 15:24:** "I shall seek the man who is himself ever seeking, who seeks to unravel the riddle of life. One whose determination is strong, who detests wickedness and delights in the good; whose heart and inner vision reach out for enlightenment. His tranquillity will remain unshaken under stress, and within his heart will be a haven of peace beyond the reach of excitement and anger. He will be a lover of wisdom and seeker of truth. He who is wise, he who knows what to do, who remains calm when others lose their self-control; he who is clearheaded under stress, who enjoys the challenge of the task, that man is Mine. He who labours uncomplainingly, who disdains to satisfy deforming lusts, whose spirit remains the same under the temptations of honours or the pressure of disgrace; he who is free from the shackles of unworthy earthly attachments, who retains his balance under praise or blame, who can shoulder his own burdens, whose spirit is calm, silent and

Segment	As Used in Video	Unabridged Quote
		strong under all circumstances; he who can bear the responsibilities of life and the obligations of love, that man is Mine. I am the God of Inspiration, I am the God of Love."

Appendix B — About The Kolbrin Bible

Newly Revealed Egyptian-Celtic Wisdom Text Offers the Knowledge of Those Who Survived Past Global Catastrophes — So We Can Live!

Millennia ago, Egyptian and Celtic authors recorded prophetic warnings for the future and their harbinger signs are now converging on 2012. These predications are contained in *The Kolbrin Bible*, a secular wisdom text studied in the days of Jesus and lovingly preserved by generations of Celtic mystics in Great Britain.

Nearly as big as the *King James Bible*, this 3600-year old text warns of an imminent, Armageddon-like conflict with radical Islam, but this is not the greatest threat

The authors of *The Kolbrin Bible* predict an end to life as we know it, by a celestial event. It will be the return of a massive space object, in a long elliptical orbit around our sun. Known to the Egyptians and Hebrews as the "Destroyer," the Celts later called it the "Frightener."

⊿ **Manuscripts 3:4** When blood drops upon the Earth, the Destroyer will appear, and mountains will open up and belch forth fire and ashes. Trees will be destroyed and all living things engulfed. Waters will be swallowed up by the land, and seas will boil.

⌐ **Manuscripts 3:5** The Heavens will burn brightly and redly; there will be a copper hue over the face of the land, 'followed by a day of darkness. A new moon will appear and break up and fall.

⌐ **Manuscripts 3:6** The people will scatter in madness. They will hear the trumpet and battlecry of the Destroyer and will seek refuge within dens in the Earth. Terror will eat away their hearts, and their courage will flow from them like water from a broken pitcher. They will be eaten u in the flames of wrath and consumed by the breath of the Destroyer.

⌐ **Manuscripts 3:10** In those days, men will have the Great Book before them; wisdom will be revealed; the few will be gathered for the stand; it is the hour of trial. The dauntless ones will survive; the stouthearted will not go down to destruction.

The Destroyer is also known today as Wormwood, Nibiru, Planet X and Nemesis. There are also troubling prophetic correlations to the future predictions of Mother Shipton's "Fiery Dragon" and the "Red Comet" warning of the Mayan Calendar 2012. While these future predictions are uncertain at best, is it possible for us to know about the Destroyer's previous flybys with a great degree of certainty.

Proven Survival Knowledge

According to historian and *Planet X and The Kolbrin Bible Connection* author Greg Jenner, "The Kolbrin Bible is the Rosetta Stone of Planet X!" This is because it's many historical accounts of past flybys, read like man-on-the-street television news interviews.

To our benefit, these accounts offer the considerable wisdom and experience of the ancients. Wisdom that helped them to survive previous flybys, and to rebuild. It goes without saying, that time-tested survival knowledge is far superior to the best guess ideas of modern pundits and experts.

This is why the ancients gifted their wisdom to a distant future generation yet unborn. So they could choose wisely. And choose we must, because the harbinger signs of their predictions point to us living today as being that generation. In a very real sense, their greatest hopes for humankind have come to rest upon our shoulders.

The Kolbrin Bible: 21st Century Master Edition Janice Manning, Editor Marshall Masters, Contributor	
Your Own World Books **Silver City, Nevada USA** yowbooks.com	**2nd Edition — May 2006** **596 Pages (Print Edition)** **384,587 Words (eBook Editions)**
Trade Paperback (8.268" x 11.693")	ISBN-10: 1-59772-005-4 ISBN-13: 978-1-59772-005-2
Adobe eBook	ISBN-10: 1-59772-006-2 ISBN-13: 978-1-59772-006-9
Microsoft eBook	ISBN-10: 1-59772-007-0 ISBN-13: 978-1-59772-007-6
Mobipocket/Kindle eBook	ISBN-10: 1-59772-008-9 ISBN-13: 978-1-59772-008-3
Palm eBook	ISBN-10: 1-59772-009-7 ISBN-13: 978-1-59772-009-0

Learn more about this book at:

www.kolbrin.com

Appendix C — How This Series Came About

Many have contributed their efforts, thoughts and ideas to the creation of this teaching series. The two principal contributors are Rebecca Jernigan and Marshall Masters. Through the experience of their lives and efforts, the story of this teaching series is told.

Rebecca Jernigan

Host of the Journeys with Rebecca Radio Show and Channel for The Elohim

journeyswithrebecca.com

Clairvoyant, author, meditation guide, and syndicated talk radio host, Rebecca is a channel for the guides she calls The Elohim, an energetic consciousness here to empower the human spirit with individual sovereignty.

Rebecca first discovered her psychic connection with The Elohim when she was 4 years old and has channeled them ever since. As an adult, she focused on her natural abilities and in 1988, was certified as a Professional Psychic. In 1994 she also became a Reiki Master Teacher in 5 disciplines.

Rebecca first became acquainted with Marshall Masters when he first appeared on her nationally syndicated radio program, Journeys with Rebecca Radio Show in October 2003. After his sixth appearance on her show in November 2006, he began researching her channeling abilities.

In October 2007, Marshall and yowusa.com co-founders Janice Manning and Jacco van der Worp, MSc, began a formal series of channeled interviews with Rebecca and The Elohim in furtherance of their research on 2012 and Planet X-related topics.

This teaching series by The Elohim was recorded the following month in a series of ten separate channeling sessions. Their messages are fully and faithfully represented in this teaching series.

Marshall Masters

Host of the Cut to the Chase Radio Show and Publisher of This Series

marshallmasters.com

Marshall Masters is an author, publisher, and the host of the Cut to the Chase Internet Radio Show. A former CNN science features news producer and the founder of The Sagan Continuation Project. He specializes in Planet X and 2012 research and began publishing his yowusa.com web site in 1999. His published books include *Planet X Forecast and 2012 Survival Guide*, *Godschild Covenant: Return of Nibiru* and *The Kolbrin Bible*.

The Virtual Serenity concept dates back to 1998 with Marshall's first effort, *Virtual Serenity: The Journey Within*, a 22-

minute relaxation video. It offers a pleasant way for viewers to diminish the effects of life's usual worries and concerns and features the Native American flute melodies of Coyote Oldman. In November 2006, he made it freely available on the Internet via YouTube.com and other video share sites. A popular 5-star favorite, it has been viewed over 250,000 times to date.

After recording numerous channeling sessions with Rebecca and the Elohim in late 2007, Marshall and yowusa.com co-founders Janice Manning and Jacco van der Worp, MSc spent months reviewing the recordings, including the ten wisdom teachings recorded in October 2007.

To help vet The Elohim, the research group asked them for predictions of major long-range Earth change and weather events that would be unknowable to modern science. The guides complied and over time, all of their predictions were accurately fulfilled.

In the first half of 2008, the yowusa.com research group also interviewed other guides through different sensitives (channelers) and these interviews corroborated many of the same concepts and warnings offered to the group during their late 2007 research efforts with Rebecca.

Then in June 2008, a critical turning point occurred. The Lexington Reservoir in Los Gatos, California was drained. The event corroborated prophetic dreams Marshall experienced each night for nearly a year, decades earlier in Texas as a young man. It was then he knew that the time had come to share these teachings, which Rebecca Jernigan had already gifted to peoples of the world. The result was the simultaneous release of this 12-part teachings series in January 2009, in the video, audio and print mediums.

To enjoy the free videos and audio versions of this teaching series, please visit:

virtualserenity.com

Printed in the United States
212538BV00003B/91/P

9 781597 720816